I0491656

VICTORY ∿ DISEASE®

Why Great Organizations Fail
and How to Innovate Before It's Too Late

ARROGANCE

COMPLACENCY

BUREAUCRACY

MICK SIMONELLI

Testimonials:

Victory Disease® transcends so many pieces of society and beholds great lessons for government, the private sector, industry and so many walks of life. I have been sharing it in my everyday activities and even have my staff walking around citing the 3 ingredients of Victory Disease – arrogance, bureaucracy & complacency.

Lieutenant General Thomas Horlander, Military Deputy,
Assistant Secretary of the Army (Financial Management and Comptrollership)

Having run one of the most transformational innovation programs in recent corporate history, Mick is one of the most respected institutions in the field. Victory Disease® is the perfect analogy to diagnose and understand what makes innovation so difficult in corporate environments. This book doesn't only helps us with this understanding; it also gives us proven and practical tools to make it happen. I wish I had read Victory Disease 10 years ago!

Moises Norena, VP of Innovation for Whirlpool, Allstate and Moen Inc.

A great read that resonated with my own learnings across many businesses and companies. There were so many relevant learnings and actions, ranging from studying history of your business and factors that led to success and failure, to the importance of ruthlessly and objectively benchmarking externally, to the recognition that innovation is fundamentally a "people game".

Bruce Brown Chief Technology (R&D,Innovation) Officer, Board Member

This book is a highly entertaining read that provides the insight necessary to diagnose the telltale symptoms of Victory Disease. Whether operating in the financial services sector, the government, or anywhere in between, Mick provides the template for leaders at all levels to understand the innovative health of their organizations. The importance of this cannot be understated as, too often, successful companies, organizations and even governments fall victim to a lack of innovation only to realize it after it is too late. Victory Disease shows us how to maintain the awareness necessary to avoid this fate.

Chris Hetz, Director of Acquisition, Defense Innovation Unit (DIU)

Mick is that rare, special breed who inspires others to think beyond boundaries . . . a man whose Army and business careers have given him rare knowledge, both about what makes organizations thrive and how to break the barriers that cause organizations to look new opportunities in the face and not recognize them. A visionary who inspires trust and creates revolutionary value in today's teams!

General (Retired) Steve Speakes, CEO, KRTC, and Former G-8, U.S. Army

With uncanny wit and wisdom Mick Simonelli explains what might be the most contagious disease among organizations today. Prescription....read twice and call him in the morning.

Brandon Rowberry, Former VP Innovation United Health Group

Victory Disease makes the decisive case for innovation. Mick Simonelli lays out in clear and easily understood terms why arrogance, bureaucracy, and complacency kills business. The comparisons to historical and world-changing events are tremendously impactful. It doesn't get more real than looking at the examples of powerful empires, history-making explorers, and megalithic U.S. institutions as Mick guides you through his case, followed by practical advice. If you are in business, large or small, you will gain insights that will empower you to be on top of your game and not fall prey to these unquestionably deadly traps.

Jason Van Camp, Best Selling Author, Deliberate Discomfort

"The ABCs of Victory Disease must be diagnosed and addressed by the most senior leaders whose personal behaviors are ultimately responsible for either infecting or curing their organizations. Leaders need to undertake deep introspection with great humility and commit to role modeling the necessary curative behaviors."

Sanjiv Waghmare, Product Management Executive

Victory Disease provides a roadmap for those starting their corporate innovation journey. For those with a few battle scars, it offers an opportunity to recharge their efforts. In both cases, this book gives practical guidance from a leader who has been on the front lines of making sustained change happen.

Mike Fitzgerald, Principal Insurance Analyst CB Insights

Mick Simonelli is a master storyteller and refreshing voice who shines a light on the one thing that even the best companies can suffer from: Victory Disease. He takes a military concept, breaks it down into a simple ABC, and then turns it into the lever for turning your innovation efforts into a success. He follows that with practical, real-world solutions and remedies to overcome Victory Disease based on his depth of experience being an innovation troublemaker in both a private and public context. In a time when innovation has never been more critical for organizations and nations to survive and thrive, Victory Disease inspires and forewarns. If you're serious about taking innovation from a buzz word to reality – or ready to become an innovation hero and troublemaker yourself – this book is for you.

Whynde Kuehn, CEO, S2E Transformation

Mick's perspective and examples serve as an excellent reminder of the need for companies to continually innovate and disrupt their own businesses—before their competitors do. Innovators can learn from the common pitfalls and productive approaches cited in Victory Disease.

Jack Weekes, retired innovation leader, Fortune 100 Corporation.

Ready for some fascinating, unique insights? Read Victory Disease by Mick Simonelli, a business system epidemiologist (!) and seasoned innovation practitioner. This mashup of storytelling, military history, and personal experience as a warrior in both the U.S. Army and business consulting worlds should be required reading for strategists in any field. Simonelli starts with many of the same facts seen elsewhere in innovation literature, but recasts them in the context of why people inevitably and rationally behave the way they do. He also points out, with country doctor clarity, the madness of leaving Victory Disease untreated.

Craig Weber, CEO Perspexion, Former CEO Celent

Of all the causes that have sunk great businesses, perhaps none other has been so salient, and yet avoidable, as the ailment of settling into past victories - of letting arrogance, bureaucracy, and complacency rob us of the imagination and creativity we need to reinvent ourselves into something better suited for the future. In Victory Disease, Mick Simonelli masterfully captures the essence of this ailment, and shows us a clear remedy for it— to let go of the past, no matter how great it was, and take hold of the future, which will inevitably look very different than the past as we press forward into the exponential changes standing before us. Read this book and follow its advice, and your business too can create a legacy that extends deep into the future.

Anthony Mills. Executive Director, Global Innovation Institute

The message of Victory Disease is long overdue. Organizations that rest on their success will fall behind or risk the painful journey of going out of business. This book is launched at a key time in history, with the toll that the Covid19 pandemic has taken on businesses, large and small. Those that are resilient and able to adapt quickly will survive. Business that overcome obstacles to innovation, while developing and sustaining a culture that expects and rewards innovation, will survive and thrive for the long-term. Mick Simonelli does a masterful job pulling together this work, relying on historical events, well-known business crises, and his personal experience, while interjecting practical viewpoints, and sprinkled with wit and humor.

Mark S. Teachout, PhD

Mick is both an instrumental and thoughtful innovator, and his work in Victory Disease is evident of a natural thought leadership and an indisputable track record in bringing sustainable innovation to life. Victory Disease is a must read for business leaders and practitioners seeking relevance and considering human-centricity by design.

Suleiman Barada; Sr. Advisor of Ecosystem Digital Transformation Unit Union of Arab Banks

VICTORY -⁄⁄- DISEASE®

Why Great Organizations Fail
and How to Innovate Before It's Too Late

By

Mick Simonelli

Victory Disease
© 2020 Mick Simonelli

ISBN:

All rights reserved. No part of this publication may be reproduced or transmitted in any form or by any means without written permission from the publisher.

Printed in the United States of America.

Contents

Introduction:
Why Victory Disease Needs a Remedy

More than seventy years ago, Japanese historians used the term *Victory Disease* to refer to their self-defeating behavior during World War II that included beliefs of invincibility and a divine right to victory. After a series of decisive early wins, the Japanese felt and acted as if they were unbeatable. Yet, the tremendous Japanese victories created a false sense of security that eventually led to their crushing defeat and their nation's humiliation. After the war, U.S. military analysts adopted the term Victory Disease, pointing to many other battles where they saw it playing a significant role. Victory Disease describes a cultural malady that Japan could have avoided if it had recognized the symptoms and acted in time. Characterized by arrogance, bureaucracy, and complacency, Victory Disease brought about the unanticipated defeat of a formidable military that saw great initial success. While military operations and strategists have since recognized the disease as a known phenomenon, this book shows how the behavior of many modern organizations mimics the symptoms of the World War II Japanese and their reluctance to change.

Victory Disease: How Great Organizations Die Without Innovation examines how successful organizations are in the midst of either succumbing to or overcoming this dreaded malady. With Victory Disease, the by-product of previous successes creates cancerous environments, a breeding ground for thriving organizations to begin developing malignant behaviors. The organizational culture becomes geared toward the status quo, which perpetuates groupthink and the belief of invincibility. Successful organizations easily fall into the trap of rewarding risk-averse behavior, where new ideas are minimized or killed to avoid disrupting previous winning ways.

But in today's hyper-innovation environment, new products, services, and solutions become the difference-makers. Modern organizations must continuously produce new value to stay on top. Yet, many established companies remain stuck in the circumstances of their current success, displaying the same predictable symptoms as did the Japanese during World War II— all the while denying their infection's severity. Barely able to look toward the future, they remain enamored with past successes— achievements that become outdated and irrelevant over time.

Unlike previous eras, the current pace of change demands new business models and practices. Successful organizations must continue to change and adapt . . . or die. *Victory Disease* examines the malaise direly affecting successful businesses and prescribes an antidote: a practical remedy for renewed organizational health and longevity.

The Innovation Journey Begins
With Some Words of Warning

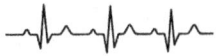

It ought to be remembered that there is nothing more difficult to take in hand, more perilous to conduct, or more uncertain in its success, than to take the lead in the introduction of a new order of things. Because the innovator has for enemies all those who have done well under the old conditions, and lukewarm defenders in those who may do well under the new. This coolness arises partly from fear of the opponents, who have the laws on their side, and partly from the incredulity of men, who do not readily believe in new things until they have had a long experience of them."

—Niccolò Machiavelli, The Prince

CHAPTER 1
Origins of Victory Disease

On the eve of World War II, the Japanese military stood strong, a powerful and dominant force. They were an efficient machine seeking to grow and expand, akin to the aggressive Amazon and Google models of our modern business era. The Japanese military possessed all the necessary capabilities to defeat any adversary, forward-thinking and poised to achieve glorious victories.

Boldly attacking Pearl Harbor on December 7, 1941, they achieved unprecedented victories over U.S. forces. Their element of surprise and gutsy initiative proved incredible; the Japanese military demonstrated ingenuity and innovation that propelled them to victory. To accomplish this feat, they took strategic risks with impressive results. In an unprecedented, covert operation, they moved six of their nine aircraft carrier groups more than 3,000 miles across the Pacific to attack Pearl Harbor—and surprised the world.

Business leaders love to use a common analogy to describe how difficult it is and how long it takes to implement change, saying large organizational initiatives are "like turning a large ship." However, the Japanese made it look easy to turn many large ships by stealthily moving six carrier groups halfway across the world—undetected. Though the large, slow-moving carrier groups were vulnerable and highly susceptible to discovery, they were masterfully maneuvered to pre-designated strike positions. The Japanese creatively hid them behind large storm systems, shadowing the disturbances in order to conceal their movement from U.S. and Allied detection. Though dangerous, this daring initiative illustrated how the Japanese would knowingly and deliberately risk international ridicule to achieve victory.

In preparation for the attack, the Japanese created many new war products and methods, making some ingenious innovations. For example, they developed special aerial torpedoes that could operate effectively in Pearl Harbor's shallow waters, modifying the torpedoes to detonate in waters where normal torpedoes wouldn't work. The Japanese developed these new torpedoes by trial and error, carrying out iterative experiments utilizing creative innovation management practices. Using test-and-learn methodologies way ahead of their time, they overcame a series of issues to create custom-made torpedoes that greatly enhanced the effects of their surprise attack.

They also leveraged their innovation expertise to develop bombs that could penetrate U.S. deck armor and inflict maximum damage. In top-secret experiments, the Japanese brought together handpicked, cross-functional teams in isolated locations to work on specific battle challenges. The U.S. term for such operations was later called *skunkworks*, a name arising from a popular comic strip character with an affinity to throw skunks into his secret *kickapoo juice*. During World War II, Skunk works® projects became a very effective method used to develop radical innovations. In American innovation literature, credit is often given to Lockheed Martin for inventing and trademarking Skunk works® projects, but the Japanese perfected the process first, making their own kickapoo juice years before the Manhattan Project used similar techniques to build the atom bomb.

World War II was the war for transformative innovation, with the Japanese the true pioneers that started the innovation race. They were the first to discover that ideas, information, and ingenuity could be combined to create winning formulas for success, and that war wasn't just about troops and direct battle.

Though the First World War brought modern weapons like tanks and airplanes into use, the Second World War saw the first true marriage of those new weapon products with creative strategies and tactics. Innovation, science, and strategy merged to yield the adaptable military approaches we still use today, ones that business has now also embraced.

As a former military transformation officer, I am amazed at how the legacy of military innovation became evident either during World War II or very soon after the fighting ended— through the many technological and strategic innovations that were introduced and improved. In addition to the launch of nuclear power during this era, the disruptive innovations that were started and/or perfected included radar, computers, jet engines, and television. All evolutionary concepts, many modern inventions can trace their roots to that very unique time.

At Pearl Harbor, thanks to the focus of those six Japanese carrier groups, the Japanese military secured a resounding success. Although they didn't destroy all the U.S. aircraft carriers, they placed the American Navy in a vulnerable position. The Japanese initiatives resulted in the destruction of much of the American Pacific fleet, giving the proud and mighty Japanese warriors victory once again.

Since the American Pacific fleet stood as the major opposing force in the Pacific, the Japanese knew that they had achieved a glorious triumph when they left the fleet severely handicapped. Overall, the Japanese sank nineteen ships, including all eight U.S. battleships, several destroyers, and many support ships. Additionally, 164 planes were demolished, with another 128 damaged. Immediately, the Americans were forced to make quick defensive decisions.

The day after Pearl Harbor, the Japanese continued their bold risk-taking by maneuvering across Thailand and attacking British-controlled Malay. In what Winston Churchill called "the worst disaster and largest capitulation in British history," the Japanese again achieved a spectacular victory over Allied forces—risky, cunning, and bold.

Once more, an innovative move had surprised the Allied forces. The British and Allied defenses on Thailand and Malay were highly regarded as impenetrable because they were so well fortified and protected. The expert positioning of British anti-armor weapons had been expected to easily repel any sea invasion. Strategists, assuming old tactics, didn't see any way an insurgency or surprise attack could defeat the Brits at Malay. The status-quo war models of the time assumed a sea assault because that's the way it had always been done or envisioned.

However, the Japanese, using new concepts for special operations, bypassed the large British anti-armor weapons altogether by assaulting from the jungle. Demonstrating an initial ability to change fighting methodology, they developed new jungle tactics and surprised the British stronghold. In business terms, they had redefined the business model for island assaults. The defending forces were completely surprised when the Japanese did not assault in a traditional sea-to-land fashion. The invasion was one of the first successful joint operations ever executed, meaning it involved naval convoy support, surprise amphibious landings, guerilla ground tactics, aircraft support, ground force air support, and ground operations. The Japanese plan creatively integrated their air, ground, and sea power. In an astounding Japanese victory, the British and Allied forces were forced to retreat and ultimately surrender. The Japanese approach was rewarded with victory in Malay, access to the Indian Ocean, and an incredible seventy thousand Allied casualties and prisoners of war. Victory celebrations were held within the military and across all of Japan.

The Japanese had successfully positioned themselves to control the Pacific. Previously known as overly cautious, the Japanese military displayed a stunning array of boldness and innovation. New tactics, new weapon systems, and novel applications for war methods spurred them on to significant early victories at the war's outset.

However, instead of continuing to evolve their military strategy and adjust their plans, the Japanese began to exhibit several risk-averse traits that made them susceptible to future battle defeats. Thus, they displayed the first outward sign of a malaise that would continue to fester from within. For example, instead of continuing to develop their tactical innovation as their Malay jungle assault so adeptly demonstrated, they became more conservative. They avoided the use of bold strategic moves and assumed their superiority would naturally continue. And, most damaging, they began to obsess about their 1,200-year history of martial prowess, allowing that glorious history of success to prevent future growth.

Japanese martial philosophy entailed both a tremendous strength and a crippling weakness. Incredible national pride marked their rich martial history. Like many organizations that take satisfaction in the annals of their past, the Japanese leadership desired to emulate their forefathers' traditions and success. Some of the military leaders were known to don the traditional garb of the samurai for ceremonies or other formal public events. They would frequently wear the historical samurai swords belonging to previously great Japanese warriors. The swords were some of the finest ever made, crafted from the choicest steel and using forging techniques from bygone days. Many of the swords were credited with cutting cleanly through a man's neck or torso with one bold stroke. And while not engaging their enemies with their traditional armor or swords, they envisioned themselves as modern embodiments of the samurai, contributing in their own way to the rich traditions of Japanese warfare.

But that strong traditional pride also had its downside. Japanese military leaders haughtily assumed they were the superior military force due to divine right. Commanders at all levels believed they were divinely inspired to victory, simply because they were Japanese, the samurai's descendants. This overemphasis on historical success led them to quickly overlook the innovative tactics and war processes that had helped them achieve initial success in the war's early stages, with credit given instead to the Japanese martial spirit. Their storied martial history became an infectious agent corrupting their ability to sustain innovation.

Like a parasitic infection that grows and morphs to corrupt an organism, expectations of victory became a cancer. This malady within the Japanese military was later called "Victory Disease"[1] by Japanese historians. The Japanese strategist Chuko Ikezaki originally coined the term, called *senshobyo* in Japanese, and Japanese post-war analysts soon adopted it as well. These historians noted that "when new winning ways continue unchanged, they become losing ways." Victory Disease quickly grew, infecting the Japanese military and culture at large. A wave of euphoria swept through Japan surrounding the initial victories. Japanese politicians, academics, and journalists exaggerated their early victories and spoke of fantastical outcomes, such as the Japanese ownership of Hawaii and the annihilation of all traces of Anglo-Saxon influence from the Pacific. Feelings of invincibility permeated the military. Victory Disease was in full swing.

CHAPTER 2
Innovation Troublemaker

I've been fighting the status quo in both the private and public sectors for over 30 years. Fortunate enough to work innovation jobs throughout my career, I rotated from military *muddy boots* leadership positions to jobs centered around new solutions and digitization. As a former Army transformation officer, I studied Victory Disease in military operations. The education of a U.S. military officer stands second to none, and I gratefully learned about numerous historical successes and failures while receiving real-world, practical experience. I was especially intrigued by the sociological impact of Victory Disease demonstrated by so many campaigns besides the Japanese in World War II. The numerous examples include Custer arrogantly charging into a hopeless situation at Little Big Horn as he was certain of victory, as well as the French invasion of Russia in 1812, where overconfident Napoleon-led troops fell victim to arrogance, resulting in the near loss of almost the entire army while trying to take Russia.

Military historical analysts James Dunnigan and Raymond Macedonia highlighted the concept of Victory Disease in their book, *Getting It Right: American Military Reforms After Vietnam to the Gulf War and Beyond*;[2] they centered their arguments on a well-documented premise: Victory Disease can easily affect a military that has seen a long history of success. As Dunnigan and Macedonia looked through the lens of history, they identified three symptoms of the disease: arrogance, established patterns of fighting (or bureaucracy), and complacency. One or all of these symptoms are usually present when a successful organization stops innovating and assumes continued success. As these symptoms develop and fester, the frequent result emerges in the unanticipated defeat of a previously successful organization.

I was fortunate to innovate in the military in numerous positions, including helping to develop and launch a new air defense system called SLAMRAAM; working as a transformation officer for the digitization of the Army; and building a brand-new army for the Republic of Afghanistan. With each challenge, I learned how incredibly difficult it becomes to introduce change into large organizations, but also how incredibly powerful innovation can be to counter Victory Disease.

One thing I've learned for sure: the status quo avoids change, hinders innovation, and frequently views innovators as troublemakers. My first big realization occurred during the new weapons development efforts of the Department of Defense (DoD). I was part of the creation of a new air defense system, eventually known as SLAMRAAM (photo below). These efforts marked my first big innovation and, subsequently, my first brush with the status quo.

SLAMRAAM firing missiles

As an Army Captain at the time, I was working with a senior Air Force non-commissioned officer. We came up with the idea for the SLAMRAAM while collaborating with defense contractors. It was a simple idea (and aren't many great innovations simple at their core?). The SLAMRAAM took two successful, existing products and combined them into one. We took the very agile Hummer vehicle and the super lethal AMRAAM air-to-air missiles and put them together. We simply placed the missiles on the back of the Hummer and thus created a new air defense vehicle. The Hummer was super reliable and could go anywhere, and the AMRAAM missiles were the best in dog-fighting operations, able to easily pick off aircraft in flight. But no one had thought of trying to use the AMRAAM missiles from the ground. But why not? This idea was the Reese's Peanut Butter Cup of weapon systems. Reese's took two great things and combined them, and so did we.

The SLAMRAAM not only comprised an innovation slam-dunk but quelled the prevalence of an existing air defense system as well: the small, ground-launched Stinger missile. While the Stinger proved mobile and very effective at close range, it was carried by a soldier. This made its range extremely limited; to engage, the operator had to move very close to the aircraft, settle for slow repositioning, and fire only one at a time. In addition, it took numerous stingers (and soldiers) deployed to support a small area.

Stinger firing

The SLAMRAAM blew away the Stinger's range by about 500 percent. Case closed. But not only that, it could fire at multiple targets quickly, whereas the existing Stingers could only fire at one. And when mounted on a hummer with a slew-to-cue turret, it was also very agile—way more so than a soldier with a missile on his shoulder. My innovation Air Force partner was a certified Stinger missile operator, so we conducted simulations of his shooting of the Stinger versus our new invention, and you can guess which performed better consistently. The new invention came out on top, hands down. For our next step we built some early stage prototypes—which performed miraculously—showing the potential to greatly increase the lethality of our air defense forces. They delivered incredible disruption potential. But . . . here's where the trouble came in . . . .

Because the SLAMRAAM proved so effective, it would disintermediate the existing Stinger ground forces. Young Captain Mick (oh . . . the naivety) thought it great news to drastically reduce the footprint of U.S. soldiers, as well as save more lives. But after a big briefing to the U.S. Army Air Defense General and his staff about the fantastic results from our early tests, the reception wasn't what I expected. In fact, the General followed me into the men's latrine, sallied up next to me, and began to talk. He told me, "Captain, that new SLAMRAAM looks good. But I've worked long and hard to get my troop numbers up to their current level, and if I lose force structure [he meant people under his command] because of you pushing this new idea, I'll break your f***ing arms." I was startled and didn't say anything as he walked away from the urinal. My exciting, lifesaving, bad-guy-killing innovation had just become a real and figurative pissing contest.

I realized the senior General was more concerned about the number of soldiers he could justify in his Army's air defense than he was in saving lives. I was disappointed that an esteemed General would put his own position above the welfare of the service. It was my first hard lesson on human nature and the negative ways some senior leaders respond to change.

I ignored his threat and kept pushing against the status quo. To quit because of threats was never a consideration for me. I would continue as long as the idea had merit, naysayers be damned, even if they were big shots. I find this attitude prevalent among most natural innovators, and it is one of the reasons we are often seen as troublemakers. My arms were never broken, but I did have to fight the bureaucracy, and along the way caused problems for some self-serving senior leaders.

Two years of marketing and pushing the SLAMRAAM followed, yet the Army still had not adopted our weapon innovation. I was forced to move on in my career to my next scheduled rotation; I watched as others took up the SLAMRAAM baton, and they too struggled with the status quo. Our new idea received the most pushback from the existing structure that managed tactical air defense, a structure built around the Stinger missile. The Stinger was already approved through the Pentagon bureaucracy (no small feat) and was funded for five years. The program managers hated the thought of destroying all that guaranteed equipment for another risky bureaucratic battle. So, the SLAMRAAM languished in uncertainty as bureaucracy prevailed. Eventually, ten long years later, the SLAMRAAM reached a tentative level of sporadic adoption and deployment throughout the U.S. military, and was also shared with our allies. But it took far too long, wasted too much time sitting on the sidelines, and fought against powers that had their own personal interests in mind.

Certainly, its tactical use has saved some lives, but not merely as many as it could (and should) have. And now, it's almost outdated and no longer transformational. The SLAMRAAM wasn't deployed quickly enough. Why? Because senior leaders in charge of air defense didn't want radical change. And also because the massive bureaucracy of the DoD made agile change very difficult.

This was all a big lesson for me. I learned that innovators have to swim upstream, sometimes maneuvering alone as scarier big fish try to eat them while they navigate the river and rocks. I learned that senior leaders don't always have the best interest of the organization in mind. They may be more concerned about their next star, or their next bonus. Surviving and possibly even thriving as an innovator and swimming upstream can prove difficult. But I also realized it was in my nature to swim upstream against the current if there is good reason to do so.

Fast forward to my career now as a business executive. I fight against Victory Disease by making its demise a centerpiece of my innovation culture-change; and as an experienced business strategist, I see Victory Disease in some aspect in almost every organization with which I work. The global impacts of Victory Disease are getting more pronounced, not less. Unfortunately, the innovation and exponential growth of our current world serves as an ever-growing catalyst for Victory Disease.

CHAPTER 3
The ABCs of Victory Disease

To understand Victory Disease, we must first understand its symptoms. Although we are witnessing Victory Disease everywhere in our modern world, the Japanese example was the first time the term was coined and shows how those symptoms interact to bring about defeat. The three major symptoms of Victory Disease—**A**rrogance, **B**ureaucracy, and **C**omplacency (what I refer to as the ABCs)—are usually present in some form. These three major symptoms will be identified in many strains as they appear in modern organizations. As cancerous cells divide and grow to move throughout a body, so Victory Disease quickly multiplies within successful organizations.

Even while the Japanese military assumed they would achieve continued success, the symptoms of Victory Disease were growing within the culture. Victory Disease is real—as real as cancer or fever. It can be easily noticed and detected in today's organizations. It wasn't just an isolated danger peculiar to the Japanese military in World War II; it now looms everywhere.

Arrogance, complacency, and bureaucracy took root within the Japanese organizational habits and beliefs and, despite a successful start, ultimately led to the utter annihilation of the Japanese military.

Similarly, Victory Disease symptoms occur in successful businesses across nearly every market. The advent of the innovation age and the sense of urgency it brings to business strategies have shown the value of examining modern business practices to avoid the dreaded ailment.

One or more of Victory Disease symptoms (arrogance,

bureaucracy, and complacency) are almost always found in organizations that are ill with victory. Please note that these usually don't present as hard symptoms, in the sense that exactitude and rigor are needed to diagnose them. More often, the symptoms appear soft or somewhat hidden, requiring an awareness of the organization's health. Victory Disease emerges subtle at first and is usually detectable only by insiders who are really paying attention. Many times, the innovative employees within the organization are first to notice it.

Much like the way cancer starts with small, barely perceptible cell corruptions, so Victory Disease symptoms also manifest as slight at first. Cancerous tumors can take months or years to develop enough for detection through tests. Victory Disease symptoms emerge the same. But just as advanced cancer symptoms eventually become obvious to all, so do the later stages of Victory Disease become grossly obvious to even external bystanders. That's why people with inside information are so essential to the early detection and cure. Internal employees become some of the most critical early detectors of the disease, with their vital role discussed in more detail later in this book.

The ABCs are not easily measured and quantified, but softer in that sense. They cannot be easily analyzed side-by-side with economic ratings or assigned business levels. For example, how does one quantify arrogance? Arrogance is associated with an attitude of superiority and assumptions of greatness. It's felt more than measured. If you meet a leader or company with arrogance, you likely won't be measuring their arrogance on a scientific scale, but you may have a feeling that they are presumptuous, that they think very highly of themselves or their ideas, often to the point of disregarding the importance of other data, facts, innovations, or mindsets. While arrogance is a psychological phenomenon, you will oftentimes see leaders use concrete, run-the-business data to support their arrogance. They may quote the number of widgets they can produce or the size of their market share, or if they're trying to launch new products, they will authoritatively point out the projected growth.

This exemplifies a limitation of Victory Disease: detecting and overcoming it is a soft science at best and an art at worst. Leaders and employees under its throes will instinctively want harder facts related to running the business. They look for concrete variables like budgets, proformas, and strategic forecasts to guide them. Organizational leaders are used to bolstering their positions with hard business or market facts. The World War II Japanese posited what they thought were key facts about their own strengths and American losses. Victory Disease wasn't on their radar. Statistics and data supporting their arrogance were the ones they used. But with all their facts and positioning, the Japanese were frequently blind-sided by the growth of their "cancer" simply because the ABCs of Victory Disease don't show up in data that leaders routinely use. And in the modern era, the disease doesn't present in proformas, balance sheets, or standard facts until it's too late; few MBA programs include strategies for young business leaders on how to avoid arrogance or complacency, or to even recognize when bureaucracy becomes excessive.

Victory Disease is so sad because it's preventable. Successful organizations often run in place, content to continue with their current stale strategy while giving lip service to innovation and ignoring the threats they observe emerging. Organizations will frequently say they are employing a fast-follower strategy that enables them to quickly copy new ideas after a competitor has invented them. But here's the rub: a fast-follower strategy requires the fast-follower company to possess a vibrant innovation and prototype program that studies the emerging ideas and rapidly reproduces them, ideally even making improvements. However, many companies that claim a fast-follower strategy really have no deliberate process at all. The fast-follower moniker merely becomes a front that hides the organization's complacency.

The established processes and operations that make successful companies efficient may inhibit innovations and new channels from growing. Bureaucratic routines and patterns cause market leaders to trudge along, attempting to incrementally improve around the margins while the flexibility and agility of emerging companies allow them to boldly achieve revolutionary products and services. Oftentimes successful companies will rely so completely on the original innovations and models that brought them success that they exclude new ideas.

The "A" of Victory Disease:
Arrogance

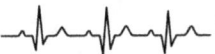

The only thing more dangerous than ignorance is arrogance.

—Albert Einstein

CHAPTER 4
Arrogance in Full Color

Arrogance is perhaps the most outrageous symptom of Victory Disease. It can be exasperating to watch as leaders and members of a failing organization behave as if nothing is wrong within their ranks. Or worse, they will continue acting superior as their team falls apart or dies around them. After their initial victories, Japanese leaders exhibited unbridled arrogance and egotism. They made prideful decisions such as renaming the Pacific the *Sea of Japan*. No other nation or leaders would recognize that the largest ocean in the world should be named after their small country. Nor did the Japanese ask anyone else, especially the other seventy-five countries or territories bordering on the Pacific Ocean, about the name change. The Japanese simply made a declaration to change the name because they felt they owned it. And by looking at the scenario through the prism of time, it's easy to see why. They felt proud coming off their amazing victories at Pearl Harbor and Malay. They defied the odds, took bold risks, and won key territories that most considered invulnerable. But their hubris went unchecked. No one could temper their swelling, victory-induced pride and nationalism. Thus, the Pacific Ocean became the Sea of Japan, at least in Japanese minds.

Even as the tide began turning in 1942, the Japanese prime minister was still under the spell of supreme overconfidence. He assembled a list of non-negotiable demands that gave Japan significant new territories and privileges, believing that victory was destined, a continual guarantee. Unfortunately, Japan's feelings of grand superiority and presumptions of success weren't based in the realities of the war environment; they were fully engrossed in arrogance. Today, this particular brand of hubris lives on in many successful organizations. Arrogance is allowed to fester and grow in many high-performing corporations and businesses—where they ignore the reality of the market and push their goods and services with the same old, tired strategy. Even in the face of imminent defeat, many are frequently rewarded. One can witness countless cases of businesses that fail to produce new products or services, and yet the leadership receives large paychecks and bonuses. As the business dies, the organization proudly ignores the warning signs.

Arrogance can comprise both an individual and organizational trait. Individuals will exhibit arrogance by displaying their own sense of self-worth and self-importance. I'm reminded of one of my former colleagues of sorts, a person who sat high in the corporate hierarchy when I led innovation in a large company. She would frequently tell the CEO that I was meddling in her organization and causing trouble, only because I was trying to launch new solutions (which, by the way, were generating over ten times return on investment). When I would visit her in her office to try to make peace, the first thing that always grabbed my attention was a life-sized painting of herself on display at the end of her large meeting table. The self-aggrandizing portrait captured her hands on her hips and a smug smile on her lips. Below her image were the words *Grande Capo,* which means *big boss* in Italian. That life-sized portrait summarized her attitude—a perceived sense of grandeur and power displayed and memorialized for all her office visitors to see. Moreover, she operated as if the world revolved around her, with no changes allowed. She insisted she knew about everything happening in her organization and that any change, no matter how big or small, had to come directly through her. Of course, that type of control proved impossible in such a large organization, and as it took a couple months' notice to squeeze onto her jam-packed calendar, that really meant very little change could ever occur. As the Innovation Officer, I was the lead change-agent, so I was forced to try to coerce her into accepting change in any way I could. And as I was forced to "kiss her ring" and reinforce how great a leader she was, I was faced with the reality of how much her individual arrogance slowed down our progress and growth.

Not just arrogance on the part of a particular leader, but organizational arrogance, sometimes called institutional narcissism, is prevalent as well. That's when an organization's culture feels a sense of overbearing pride or superiority. Unlike the *Grande Capo (big boss)* that is limited to one person, organizational arrogance causes the entire organization to stop learning and asking questions. Groupthink becomes the common practice when pride and organizational righteousness rule the culture.

And what happens to those who don't think like the group? When curious about other options outside the groupthink, independent and creative minds are seen as troublemakers and rarely rewarded for their attempts at innovation. Organizational arrogance is damaging to independent thinkers as they find it difficult to get by-in from fellow employees who want to avert the *troublemaker* label. If arrogance, whether individual or organizational, isn't tempered with humility and introspection, it quickly becomes a malignant growth that causes great harm over time.

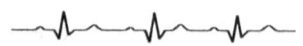

Practical Reflection: Michelin Run-Flat Tires

A real-world example of the difficulty of detecting Victory Disease is illustrated in the story of the tire giant Michelin and their expansion into run-flat tires. In the 1990s, Michelin enjoyed the status of a very successful tire industry juggernaut. It was then, at the height of their many victories, that their leadership came up with a seemingly useful innovation called the *run-flat tire*. The run-flats seemed like a very good idea at the time. *Run-flats* were tires that could continue running for a hundred miles or more, even when flat, without requiring immediate repair. They were also hailed as a safety enhancement because they would have fewer blowouts, and hence, fewer accidents would occur. Michelin, considering themselves an innovative giant, launched a full-scale effort to bring their run-flats, called the PAX system, to market. They wanted a winning product to revolutionize the tire industry. The challenge lay in their approach.

In every business case study you will see that analyzes the Michelin PAX run-flat launch, findings fall on the hard science facts of why the run-flat tires failed and usually point to the lack of service garage support to replace the tires when damaged. Or they will cite the excessive costs of the tire repair, highlighting the necessity of frequent tire replacement and purchase because of the lack of service stations that could service them. Finally, they say that the ultimate loss of consumer confidence signaled the death mark. But none of those issues pinpoint the root cause of failure. All those give valid reasons *why* it failed, but the *root cause* of failure was arrogance among the Michelin leaders who were pushing it.

They were so convinced they had a winner, and so sure of their continued dominance in the tire market, that they failed to take the necessary steps to ensure a winning product. Company press releases unduly patted themselves on the back with statements such as, "In simple terms, we have reinvented the tire." Their CFO touted, "They perform better in every respect. In ten years, there won't be any other kind of tire except PAX." And the company's CEO, Edouard Michelin himself, said, "We consider it . . . as important as the introduction of radials, if not more important." No business scale exists to measure arrogance, but statements like those imply a sense of inevitable success, as if they couldn't lose. And with feelings of invincibility come the inevitability of losses.

The best organizations are those that take humble approaches to new products, and conduct tests and pilots to vet through all the risks. They test and learn, and then apply those learnings in a rapid fashion to move forward. Where arrogance prevails, large assumptions are made regarding success. In Michelin's case, they assumed that everyone else in the tire ecosystem would accept their new idea. Though perhaps a very good innovation, it was executed poorly due to arrogance, leaving hundreds of thousands of tire owners without a viable service solution. My family had run-flat tires on our Odyssey minivan (ah, yes, the minivan days) back in 1996, so I was personally part of the debacle. I was one of those customers who experienced the emotional rollercoaster: grateful at first to have tires that could continue running flat, and then regretful I had tires with no reasonable service options, holding my breath should something go wrong.

Sick organizations usually think they are much better than reality reveals and reflect those thoughts through their people and culture. While a positive trait, confidence can manifest into arrogance and thus provide a foothold for Victory Disease to undermine the organization. Michelin's run-flat tire experience offers a prime example of arrogance, one of the ABCs of Victory Disease that frequently impairs a healthy organization.

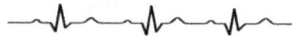

While exuding both individual and organizational arrogance in their battle plans following Pearl Harbor, the Japanese flagrantly ignored the signs and events that should have encouraged strategy changes. Key military leaders believed that *divine right* would carry them through to their ultimate war goal, completely discounting the critical roles of innovation and risk taking, despite the early innovation successes.

At a major military strategic conference in Japan shortly after Pearl Harbor, speakers bragged about the remarkable skill of Japanese warriors, the superior traits of Japanese military units, and how Japan's time for military dominance had finally arrived. Although the conference was purposed to refine strategic thinking, it turned into a series of self-congratulatory presentations about Japanese military greatness. One speaker's anchor statement echoed the informal conference theme: "The Rising Sun will crush American and British forces everywhere they exist, because we are superior." Strategists devoted very little of the conference to discussing the use of new strategies and how to continue to evolve new battle innovations.

The excessive sense of military self-worth reached such extreme heights that military commanders were considered demigods. Military leaders became overly focused on the innate superiority of the Japanese warrior and ignored the impact of ingenuity. Japanese Prime Minister General Tojo stated, "Australia and New Zealand are now threatened by the might of the Imperial Japanese forces, and both of them should know that any resistance is futile."

Japanese military leaders literally believed they were children of the gods and that the Emperor was their divine father. Military officers were taught they were indomitable and could not be defeated. If you're a god, any thought of losing gets immediately banished. The samurai culture so reinforced these beliefs that they thought their divine invincibility could overcome any challenges, even death itself. Like an infectious disease grows and corrupts enough cells to affect an organism, Japanese arrogance began to corrupt follow-on military operations.

For example, in the strategic area of Guadalcanal, the Japanese brashly conducted a frontal assault on fortified U.S. Marine positions. In a move reminiscent of Custer during his last stand when he and his men vainly rode full speed into a Native American stronghold, the Japanese ran headlong into the breach, expecting to win. Despite the success of the special tactics as used in Thailand and Malay, the Japanese chose to abandon their previous ingenuity and imagination during the Guadalcanal approach. Their leader, Commander Ichiki, was convinced that martial superiority was enough to win the day. His brazen frontal assault was easily defeated in what became an early tide-turning win for Allied forces in Guadalcanal. After the battle, only 128 out of a thousand Japanese soldiers survived.

Ichiki's arrogance, and that of his fellow officers, was based on a quasi-mystical faith in their martial abilities that transcended the reality of the battlefield. Ichiki believed, as did most Japanese commanders, that they would succeed because they were pre-destined to win.

One of the casualties of that battle was Commander Ichiki himself, who apparently committed suicide after realizing the magnitude of his defeat. Ritual suicide (called *seppuku*) is a form of Japanese apologetic suicide wherein the leader disembowels himself with a short blade. Suicide after failure became a pattern during the war, further inhibiting the Japanese military's ability to recognize and learn from their losses. In this case, Ichiki was even promoted posthumously to Major General.

Leaders, expecting to prove victorious, committed suicide to escape dishonor when they fell short of success. Failure was not allowed. While the Japanese culture might have considered suicide honorable, it prevented them learning from failure or developing an alternative strategy that would succeed. Instead, suicide reinforced the lesson that the punishment for failure was death.

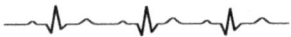

Practical Reflection: The Horrible Cost of Perfection

Perfectionism and fear of failure frequently arise as enemies of innovation. New ideas and inventions must be tested for learning to result. And during the testing and piloting stage of the innovation process, failure happens frequently. It's a natural outcome of trying new ideas.

For the over 500 innovations I've launched, many of the best successes came from failing initially and then applying the lessons learned in a different way. A best practice I use entails conducting post-mortems or after-action reviews after launching a large new initiative or entrepreneurial endeavor. It's a great way to review the original goal, what went well, what didn't go well, and how the idea or business should proceed. However, not all organizations are open to admitting failure or to changing processes after failure.

One such example of a company that wasn't ready to learn from after-action reviews was a large U.S. bank I worked with a couple of years ago.

In one of their initiatives, they wanted to explore the use of available housing data to grow their mortgage portfolio. To accomplish this, they performed several tests using publicly available mortgage data to make new offers on mortgages. After a three-month period and five different tests, none of the tests had achieved enough revenue lift to justify a full-blown pilot.

I conducted one of their first after-action reviews. All the key participants and leaders were present as I explained the ground rules. No blame and no pulling rank were allowed—only open exploration of the root causes of our successes and failures—so we could identify ways to pivot and improve.

However, during the review question, "What went wrong?" we all realized that the Senior VP of Mortgage did not really want to explore the topic. She completely missed the learning value of the review and blustered loudly, "Learnings are fine, but everyone in my organization is graded on their success and ability to grow revenue."

A few minutes later, when a junior leader spoke of not having achieved the right preparatory time frame for mortgage renewal during the test, the senior VP demanded, "Who failed to achieve the correct offer lead times? We can't allow that to occur!"

Everyone fell silent. The after-action review took a quiet, non-productive turn after the participants saw that blame would be assigned and failure punished, with no opportunity for open discussion and learning. The VP had the same mindset as the unforgiving Japanese in World War II.

However, her auto loan senior VP peer, who was also present for the review, gleaned some interesting information. During our failed tests, we had discovered correlations between the behaviors of various mortgage holder types that we were able to use for great benefit in other parts of the organization.

We learned that over 50 percent of our targeted home mortgage population had also purchased a car within six months of purchasing a new home. And, of those who purchased a new car, about 60 percent of them financed their new car. We took this information and built a new innovation test, this time without the senior mortgage officer's participation. This excited the auto loan department, and they were able to spin off a successful initiative that capitalized on that information. In the new test for auto loans related to house mortgages, they gained a remarkable 10 percent revenue-lift of our test population. When the bank extrapolated these gains across their large market, it resulted in new auto loans totaling more than $100M, a remarkable bump.

This auto loan correlation would never have been discovered without the failed mortgage initiative—and would not have been pursued to begin with if the auto loan senior VP had maintained the same "kill the failure" attitude of the senior mortgage officer. After failure in one bank department occurred, a lesson from that failure and openness to new information helped another department achieve success.

Though it may seem counterintuitive, it's true: failure—and gleaning lessons learned from it—can result in unexpected success.

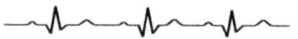

CHAPTER 5
The Japanese Z Plan

Japan's World War II Victory Disease caused them to abandon their innovative tactics and use the old, repetitive means of fighting, including the same lines of communication. In modern organizations, "the way we've always done it" signals a clear manifestation of harmful arrogance. Any avenues for a cure are shut down if an organization continues to repeat the same actions with no thought toward improvements. And when the organization defends those actions because of history or rank, or due to something unrelated to utility, that mindset is symptomatic of an organizational sickness. Arrogance must constantly be challenged, and when not, the lack of introspection and humility becomes a barrier to change as the organization assumes its ways are already perfected. Arrogance encourages routines and business practices to become unmovable monuments within the organization. Then those monuments become stale and predictable, frequently causing individuals to lose touch with their best and highest purpose. In the case of the Japanese, many of their processes, tactics, and strategies became stale—disengaged from the ever-changing battlefield environment.

"The way we've always done it" was particularly harmful in the areas of information and communication. Because the Japanese became set in their ways, they disregarded communications security and military intelligence. To make matters worse, they assigned the least inspired and lowliest officers to their intelligence units. This produced catastrophic results as the U.S. Navy and Army quickly deciphered Japanese war communications, subsequently used to anticipate Japan's battle plans. By relying on old methods and ignoring change, the Japanese gave away critical intelligence and, inadvertently, lost strategic advantage.

One such disastrous example lies in Japan's refusal to change their battle plans for the *Z Plan*. The Z Plan was the Japanese all-out plan for a major concentrated assault on U.S. forces around the Philippines. They planned to frontally attack Allied forces by both air and land. They wanted it to be a major defining victory, like Pearl Harbor. Unfortunately for the Japanese, the Z Plan was compromised when the plane of their key planner, General Fukudome, went down over hostile territory; he (and the Z Plan) were captured by guerillas. When Fukudome was somehow released by the guerillas, he was found uninjured but missing the plan. Because of the missing plan, it should have been a top priority to change it.

Though Fukudome returned to Japan in disgrace, the Japanese did not change or scrap the plan. Incredibly, even though the plan was clearly compromised, their arrogance overrode good decision-making. The Japanese instead focused on the Bushido-inspired question of whether Fukudome's capture had brought him dishonor or whether capture by guerrillas even counted as true capture. The real question should have centered around how to learn and improve from the reality of potentially compromised codes: "What went wrong and how can we improve it?" But instead, much debate by Japanese senior leadership raged concerning whether Fukudome had dishonored the warrior way. The wrong question was then asked: "Should Fukudome die?"

Regarding the question of whether he should be executed, Fukudome refused to cooperate and rebuffed the hints from the Japanese high command to commit suicide. The Emperor, after private deliberation, made a most unusual decision, actually deciding to promote Fukudome to eliminate rumors of his dishonor among the military ranks. But the entrenched bureaucracy had caused them to use compromised intelligence coding methods, and arrogance prevented them from realizing it.

Meanwhile, the United States' General MacArthur came into possession of the Z Plan and had copies sent to Admiral Nimitz and key commanders, who started planning accordingly. Thanks to arrogance, they had the Japanese playbook.

Assuming martial superiority and still ignoring the plan's compromised secrecy, the Japanese launched their Z Plan offensive with very few changes. The results? Predictably disastrous—as the Allies leveraged their inside knowledge. Of the mission's 430 aircraft carrier planes launched, only a paltry thirty-five remained post-battle. The outcome of the Z Plan proved so costly and embarrassing that Japan's military had to completely hide it from the Japanese population. They covered it up with positive propaganda, fragrantly lying about a glorious Japanese victory. In reality, wave after wave of Japanese aircraft were shot down in flames prior to reaching their objective. An epic failure for the Japanese and one of the worst manifestations of the disease had reached fruition. While the Japanese propagandized about a victory that day, the Americans referred to the fateful scenario as the Great Turkey Shoot, reveling in how easy they shot Japanese planes from the sky when the plan "rested in their pocket."

Swollen with pride from previous victories, the Japanese command leadership continued to arrogantly eschew change in favor of their established patterns, allowing the Allies to disrupt operations of their once dominant and successful force. That rigidity inhibited new ideas and fresh thinking, causing the loss of strategic agility.

CHAPTER 6
Arrogance in Action

At the core of people's arrogance lies a thinking bias that causes them to believe they are better than they really are; yet this mindset is not without consequences. Psychologists have termed arrogant overconfidence as the Dunning-Kruger effect, so named for the researchers who discovered it. Dunning and Kruger found that some persons were incapable of self-awareness, remaining blind to their actual level of competence or incompetence. They found that arrogant people can possess a blind spot of self-awareness whereby they don't realize they're not nearly as infallible as they suppose. Due to their blind spot, others will view them as pompous or arrogant while the individual remains in the dark to this perception.

The Dunning-Kruger effect isn't limited to just individuals but infects entire organizations as well; in fact, its effect is illustrated in the airlines industry. The major airline carriers are consistently ranked in the most hated company category year after year (Southwest and JetBlue excluded). Travelers cite the cabin service, extra fees, poor communication, and poor customer experience as the reasons for their anger. Almost everyone has seen or heard the horror stories of customers who were dragged off planes or had their seats downgraded without apology or explanation—and they rightly loathe that sort of treatment. Yet the airlines continue to operate with impunity while ignoring the unhappiness they are causing.

As a frequent flyer, I see it all the time. In fact, it's embedded in their rewards structures. Most airlines have even created a superstructure class ranking, treating travelers differently based on their status. Because I fly frequently, I get special treatment on two airlines and have witnessed how differently I'm treated compared to other passengers; yet it's mostly because of an artificial status designation. While I receive free upgrades, boarding and baggage privileges, and other niceties, infrequent coach travelers are often treated callously. It's easy to see people's anger towards the airlines just based on how differently they're treated in their faux class rankings. The major airline brands have created new class structures that exist only in their world—pecking orders that smack of privilege and hierarchy.

When airline employees' perceived authority is somehow challenged with a confrontation, they show their customer disdain with aggressive bureaucracy and/or policy justification. Yet it illustrates a rotten, arrogant way to treat customers that the major airlines don't think twice about. For the time being at least, those major airlines enjoy a monopoly of sorts, which keeps Victory Disease at bay. But underneath the surface, a bubbling discontent is churning that will someday manifest and disrupt their business model. In customer experience surveys, nontraditional airlines such as Southwest and Jet Blue are the recipients of customer goodwill due to their attitude deviations from the other airlines. As these smaller, more innovative airlines expand their routes, more travelers will select them as an option. The improved customer experience will grow the nontraditional airlines to a point of challenging the arrogance of the traditional airline models, resulting in the ultimate disruption of the major airline brands.

My field of financial services and the banking industry are also rich with success and arrogance. Major banks and their leaders, especially those in the "too big to fail" camp, are constantly exhibiting their feelings of invincibility. A couple of recent public examples include the Bank of America debit card fee in 2011, as well as the Wells Fargo fraud case in 2016. These cases are great in illustrating the negative outcomes of arrogance.

In 2011, Bank of America decided to charge debit card holders a $5 monthly fee for using their debit cards.[3] In my opinion, it represented a very uncreative and insensitive leadership decision. They desired more revenue so decided to charge for a previously free service. In essence, a pure money decision spawned a new business policy designed to raise large revenue through charging the many debit customers a small fee, with the crass assumption the customers would just accept the change. This reveals the *modus operandi* of arrogant organizations—the ability and gumption to make unilateral decisions without care for their customer. But in this case, the customer revolted. An online petition generated over 300,000 signatures, and numerous Facebook and other media posts released a wave of anger. Bank of America was quickly forced to change their policy and withdraw the fee. Yet the original debit fee exemplified a tactical money grab to eke more revenue from their customers. And if you look at their fee structure since then, you'll see they merely found other ways to gouge their customer. They didn't recognize their arrogance nor fundamentally change the way they do business. They merely stopped one action, which was detected and spotlighted, and shifted their profit-making approach to more subtle increases.

The Wells Fargo fraud offers another example of big bank misbehavior; in this case, the arrogance of leadership was on full display. In 2016, Wells Fargo agreed to pay $190M to settle a fraud case in which they were accused of pushing checking account customers into other credit, savings, and online accounts that generated additional fees.[4] Management pressured low-wage workers to achieve unrealistic targets and ignored the alleged two million bogus accounts that were created. The result was the opening of millions of fraudulent checking and savings accounts for unaware customers. Allegedly 5,300 employees were involved and subsequently fired.

However, the real arrogance came from the CEO and leadership of Wells Fargo who created a climate that caused so many fraudulent activities to occur. When that scale of fraud happens, senior leaders are responsible, no matter how many employees they make the scapegoat. Senior leaders create the climate and dictate the ethical standards for their employees' work. However, the job of not a single senior Wells Fargo executive was reported terminated over the matter.

While testifying before the Senate, their CEO was noncommittal and arrogant. He was asked, would he commit to investigate whether the fraud began in earlier years?

"I can't tell you that today," he replied.

Did he learn about the fraud before reading about it in the *Los Angeles Times*?

He answered, "I don't remember the exact time frame."

Did the bogus accounts hurt customers' credit scores?

He responded, "I don't know the algorithms."[5]

It illustrated denial at its worst. The CEO reportedly made $20M that year while his customers were ripped off and their credit scores damaged. In my opinion, it was chronic arrogance on display.

CHAPTER 7
Bushido Arrogance

Japan's Victory Disease reached peak acceleration through an especially critical aspect of their arrogance—*Bushido*. As a strong, underlying cultural belief in Japan, the concept of Bushido was based on two key convictions: first, that Japan knew the only true and right way; and second, that superior beings had developed ancient Japanese warrior ways for use *now* without any changes necessary. The Japanese military reacted under the great influence of this warrior way, believing it signified the ancient, unwritten code of the samurai that generation after generation of Japanese leaders adhered to and passed down. Thus, they brought Bushido to the forefront in all their decisions and strategies.

Historians dispute the exact date when Bushido originated, but most agree the samurai had embodied it for centuries. The philosophical principles of Bushido provided the guidelines of the warrior way, and at face value posed no problem. In fact, Bushido itself was quite honorable. Depending on the Japanese teacher, Bushido encompassed seven to nine principles embodying courage, benevolence, honor, and loyalty—all valuable traits for a modern soldier as well as an ancient samurai. Martial arts mastery accompanied the principles. Expectations for knowing the tools of one's martial trade and carrying them out to perfection were all part of Bushido. It proved a powerful and amazing way for military leaders to behave. What made the Bushido principles so harmful was their basis in a sense of complete self-righteousness. A smug overconfidence accompanied their performance—and stifled all who desired to deviate from their swaggering acts of bravado.

Bushido produced the strong side effect of imparting an

entitled sense of victory to the Japanese military. Steeped in a long history of tradition and ritual, the path of Bushido was considered the only path to success, and those not adhering to Bushido were deemed inferior.

All of Japan's opponents were, therefore, inferior as they did not adhere to Bushido. In the minds of many Japanese military leaders, Bushido presented the *only* way, not just an alternative. In that respect, their rigidity became an obstacle against change and innovation. Just as many of today's successful organizations think their way of success proves the only way and stubbornly stick by it, so too was the Japanese Bushido mentality thought superior. Bushido exuded so much power during World War II that the civilian sector of Japan was also indoctrinated. Bushido spread to influence everything within Japan in a way the West found hard to understand. As an island and thus closed off, Japan saw the concepts of Bushido become very intense and influential. In the people's eyes, the Emperor actually became the supreme being, replacing the lords of old. And as a supreme being, the Emperor must receive reverence and obedience at all costs. Not only did this signify a strong underpinning of arrogance, but the decisions emanating from the Emperor were also extremely hierarchical in nature; opinions below the Emperor simply didn't matter much.

The classic Japanese book on Bushido, titled *Hagakure*, was written in the early 18th century. Quite ominously, it seemed to forecast Victory Disease as it begins with the words, "Bushido is a way of dying." In fact, *Hagakure* became the bible for the Imperial Army and Navy, so much so that Japanese soldiers and sailors were taught Bushido as part of their official training. Copies of *Hagakure* were given to the Imperial forces before their deployment to war. Troops were expected to live and die according to the principles of Bushido that *Hagakure* promoted. As Bushido became such a powerful force for Japanese soldiers at that time, the *Hagakure* effectually inspired a whole generation of Japanese to revive their pride in ancient samurai ways. Yet that wasn't all; the negative and perhaps more powerful effect lay in their seeming intoxication, even delusional state about the samurai code—their belief that it was the *only* way. And since they possessed the only way, many believed they were destined to win. And if they didn't win? It was their fault. And if it was their fault, then they deserved to die.

Unchecked arrogance usually emerges in some calamitous form; it can't stay hidden. And that paints the picture of the Japanese challenge. As the war progressed, Japanese arrogance worsened, with the cancerous cells of overconfidence multiplying as quickly as the *Hagakure* books were printed. Despite seeing plenty of evidence that the Allies were deploying formidable forces to counter their strategy, the Japanese military continued on their dangerous path of assumed superiority—ignoring warning signs and failing to modify their approach.

The Japanese Emperor Hirohito witnessed the mindset at a party when some of his senior commanders performed a ritualistic victory dance symbolizing Japan's ongoing victory. Although upheld as divine and definitely a part of the arrogance problem, the Emperor personally recognized his military's overconfidence with some concern, stating, "The fruits of victory are tumbling into our mouths too quickly." For at least a moment, even the divine Emperor recognized their overconfidence.

General Yamashita, a senior leader in the Japanese military who oozed that same overconfidence, stated, "The only words I spoke to the British commander in the negotiations for the surrender of Singapore were 'All I want to hear from you is yes or no.' I expect to put the same question to MacArthur." His belief that victory was predestined emerged of course premature; he was under the influence of the pride and a sense of superiority that was then Bushido.

Because Bushido clearly defined a warrior's characteristics and traits, no wiggle room existed for deviating from the age-old traditions. Their use of shallow water torpedoes, new deck-penetrating bomb inventions, and bold tactics at Pearl Harbor received no credit in helping achieve the victories; all the cutting-edge advances were deemed anomalies. Innovation and ingenuity were considered an insignificant part of battle, with all the successes and victories instead attributed to natural Japanese superiority.

While under Victory Disease, Japan continuously neglected to see failure as a learning event. Instead, failure was dishonorable, a reason to die. After all, the *Hagakure* dictated that Bushido is a way of dying. Ritualistic suicides became a regular practice after failure and prevented the Japanese from learning from their mistakes. What a toxic way to keep from making mistakes or to learn from them—just kill yourself and create a climate of death for failure. People couldn't grow in the world of *do or die* where risk-taking proved lethal. Yet Japan didn't see that as a problem. No, the Japanese believed they were winning precisely because of their warrior way. They were too far immersed in their arrogance to even glimpse it. And Bushido did offer some very positive aspects grounded in tradition and honor, including a long martial tradition of excellence. But despite compelling some very powerful positive forces, Bushido also played another, even more sociological role. It fostered organizational arrogance that was, and is, one of the key components of Victory Disease.

Organizational arrogance occurs when the arrogant opinions of individuals or groups influence the greater culture to assume an inherent superiority, just because they've previously achieved something noteworthy. Organizational arrogance such as the Japanese malaise entails an understudied aspect of organizational decline, largely because arrogant organizations do not allow or believe they warrant studies of their arrogance. Ironically, their arrogance is what doesn't allow honest assessments of their climate and culture.

They suffer from what sociologists call *grandiose narcissism*, defined as an organization with an inflated sense of its organizational worth, overconfidence in making decisions, and an inability to learn from its mistakes. The organization suffering from arrogance malaise sees itself as perpetually successful. Its top brass usually has measures and markers that support their sense of continued success. Very similar to an arrogant leader who surrounds him or herself with *yes* people, the arrogant organization surrounds itself with measures and structures that reinforce its perception of self-excellence.

Like the Japanese unacceptance of failure in World War II, so anything that challenges the belief of continued excellence is shunned. Whereas the Japanese ritually killed their failures, modern arrogant organizations ritually fire their innovators. I frequently list my official title as "Innovation Troublemaker" because that is how the status quo sees me. Innovators who assume the risk of new ideas in arrogant organizations are usually the first ones fired or demoted when failure occurs. Failure doesn't even have to occur; merely the risk of failure is enough to attack the change agent. And because innovation is risky by nature, failure always remains a possibility. So, innovators in modern organizations infected by arrogance sit in perilous job positions. As a consultant who works at the strategic level, I see first-hand far too many competent and well-intentioned innovators receive the ultimate punishment of an organizational culture that thinks itself beyond failing by any means. And after a few innovators are fired (or Generals die through seppuku), people simply stop taking risks—and innovation ceases.

The "B" of Victory Disease:
Bureaucracy

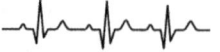

Bureaucracy is the death of all sound work.
—Albert Einstein

CHAPTER 8

Bureaucracy Illustrated

"Established patterns of fighting and routines"—that's how Japanese analysts originally defined bureaucracy decades ago. As I've observed Victory Disease across America's most successful organizations, I've expanded Victory Disease bureaucracy to include *Webster's Dictionary* definition: "a specialization of functions, adherence to fixed rules, and hierarchy of authority as they're used in modern organizations." Bureaucracies have grown since World War II and, in a very real sense, can be found everywhere.

To most Americans, the vices of bureaucracy are self-evident. Bureaucracies entail rigid and impersonal structures that squash creativity. While the professional climate demands more and more personalized treatment, bureaucracy doesn't acknowledge individual needs and differences, preferring to treat everyone the same—even if doing so proves ridiculous at face value. Bureaucracy is the Transportation Securities Administration demanding that a handicapped, 4-year-old child walk through a medical detector without his braces. This absurdity results from a TSA policy seeking to randomly search people regardless of risk profiles or groups. Bureaucracy is also the phone service of a well-known bank routing a customer to the same non-responsive, dead-end phone tree categories that are supposed to help customers (or, more frequently, save money) but demoralize and frustrate them instead.

Nonetheless, bureaucracy is a necessary evil in successful organizations. Whereas an organization doesn't always exhibit the other two symptoms of Victory Disease, arrogance and complacency, some form of healthy or unhealthy bureaucracy is always present in any successful organization. It can manifest in as little bureaucracy as the two-person company dividing responsibilities to avoid duplication of effort; or it can show up in as much bureaucracy as a company's process libraries and lock-step roles for every step of each process. In many cases, bureaucracy promotes efficiency and order, ensuring that organizations run like smooth, oiled machines. Imagine trying to order something online without some sort of system and rules. Operating without bureaucracy would prove very difficult, especially in complicated or larger organizations. However, the same systems and rules that help ensure efficiency can often prevent real innovation from happening.

A bureaucracy is often exhibited through formal procedures and standards, typically having a clear division of labor and hierarchy of authority. The term *bureaucracy* was originally coined by French economist Jacques Claude de Gournay, who literally called it "government by desks." I must admit I'm a bureaucracy-hater because of its impact on change and innovation. I intuitively make the habit of snaking out harmful bureaucracy a key part of my profession, but it also spills over into all aspects of my life where I encounter and target silly bureaucratic processes. I just go nuts when I get caught in a circular loop of an organization that sends me back and forth from department to department without ever really helping me. It reminds me of the poor state of U.S. intelligence during my time in Afghanistan (see my book *Riding a Donkey Backwards Through Afghanistan*) where the right hand didn't know what the left hand was doing, illustrating a bureaucracy that put Americans and their allies in danger. As De Gournay first observed over 300 years ago, bureaucracy proves a serious impediment to growth.

Bureaucracy is composed of hierarchy, rules, and specialization. Each of these elements can hurt innovation and, if left to their own devices, can grow into innovation-killing systems. For example, hierarchy is a bureaucratic necessity that's effective for running a business, but it's horrible for innovation. Great ideas don't have rank, and no positive correlation exists between high-ranking leaders and great ideas. In fact, in my experience the opposite tends to be the case. Many times, those persons wholly encumbered with institutional knowledge are least likely to conjure up transformative thoughts precisely *because* they know all the limitations involved. Therefore, the most hamstrung thinkers are frequently the people in charge of the organization, and unfortunately, those same hamstrung leaders usually control the budgets.

Budgets are allocated according to an incremental plan, which is tied to some sort of results. So unless an initiative gets run through the plan, it fails to get funded. On one hand, plans are notoriously stodgy and old-fashioned, predicated on what has already been done and is known. On the other hand, future innovations are not predictable or quantifiable—and are thus excluded from most budgets. Essentially, a bureaucracy becomes a spider web of rules and systems that takes hold of new ideas and entangles them in sticky threads of requirements until they're suffocated and wrapped so tight that they sit paralyzed.

In my field of financial services, numerous insurance companies had the idea to launch usage-based insurance. Also known as pay-as-you-drive or mile-based auto insurance, a usage-based model stipulates that the amount a customer pays depends upon the type of vehicle used measured against time, distance, behavior, and place. In other words, they watch your driving and reward you based on how you drive. But while many successful insurance companies broached the idea, their bureaucracy ate away the guts of the innovation. I watched quite a few major insurance companies initially kill the idea of usage-based insurance. The risk of the consumer not liking the extra attention on their driving scared away their large marketing departments. The corporate lawyers raised the concern that customers might try to cheat the system. And the overall costs of testing the new endeavor were reasoned as too high in the face of an unpredictable outcome. In successful bureaucracies the status quo is always defended, and new ideas are usually wrapped up, suffocated, and killed.

These established bureaucracies caused the companies to drop the usage-based insurance programs in favor of more predictable budgetary items such as upgrading their websites or incrementally improving existing products. Most insurance companies entertaining the idea became stuck in the bureaucratic Victory Disease malaise of risk-avoidance and are still playing catchup. Only Progressive® was able to overcome the bureaucratic hurdles to launch a usage-based program in 2008, and has greatly benefitted from taking that risk ever since. Projections indicate that 70 percent of insurance providers will offer usage-based insurance by 2021, and so insurance companies are now scrambling to claim a smaller share of the market than Progressive already holds. Meanwhile, these bureaucratic insurance organizations are falling further and further behind as new, radical initiatives such as driverless cars and networked vehicle computers are closing in hard with intense business model pressure.

Bureaucracy isn't bad. It's just that bureaucracy in large doses proves inconducive for innovation and change. Rules and regulations—the necessary evils within modern markets and organizations—are set in place to promote standardization, fairness, and consistency. But rules and regulations continuously stifle and asphyxiate creativity and spontaneity. The best way to overcome bureaucracy beset with rules and regulations is to bypass or reduce it. If an organization can innovate in spaces that haven't yet seen heavy governance, more freedom of movement still exists, and freer movement produces better results. For example, the ability to regulate ridesharing wasn't yet formed when Uber launched its innovation. The concept of a connective company using a peer-to-peer business model to enable collaborative ridesharing was foreign to regulators. Fortuitously, the innovative sharing model was positioned in a grey area of regulation so it couldn't be squashed. Uber was in front of the regulation so the rules didn't hinder the new launches, and now regulation is trying to catch up (and hopefully it never does).

As an important element for established organizations, bureaucratic specialization has become a double-edged sword. With no specialization of functions, the industrial revolution would have tragically derailed. With specialization of functions, workers can each possess a specific area of expertise and work both individually and as a team to manage something that one person alone could never do. The essential element of specialization pervades most modern organizations, with specialized employees possessing the required operational expertise to supply the product or service. For example, in my field of financial services, if an organization provides auto insurance and has done so successfully for a while, they will have specialized employees that speed along the process of acquiring and serving auto insurance customers. Their sales team will market and sell the product, licensed auto insurance agents will interact with the customer, underwriters will analyze and assume the risk, accountants will manage the finances, and leaders will oversee and understand it all. This specialization proves very efficient and necessary to run the successful auto insurance business. Yet that very specialization and success will also hamper innovation and change. Why? Because new ideas won't necessarily fit into the specialized roles within the organization.

If you look at any of the current market share leaders for insurance, you'll find they have specialization and operational expertise to efficiently run their business. Yet when they explore new methods and technologies, their operational expertise impedes their ability to adopt new ideas. The successful sales team is unable to envision new techniques for marketing. The insurance agents are unable to stretch their thinking outside their current operations. Insurance agents make their livelihood from selling insurance, so they will not embrace any ideas that supplant that role. And while many new auto insurance ideas don't require agents, somehow human agents maintain a stranglehold on insurance processes. In fact, some of the best ideas involve automatic and streamlined offerings where insurance is issued without having to interact with a single person at the insurance company. And underwriters, the mathematical experts on assuming risk, are used to grouping and evaluating risk in certain ways, so when a big data solution comes along that doesn't require the underwriters' current processes, they are confused and hesitant to accept the idea.

Leaders of traditional organizations want to play it safe by building on the success of the organization, so instead of embracing the more radical (and more effective) ways of innovating, they err in favor of incremental changes to the existing methods. Victory Disease causes leaders to prefer the guaranteed routes of small change rather than the riskier paths requiring more complex change.

In bureaucracy, good ideas are rejected in favor of processes. Most insurance carriers will reject ideas surrounding automation such as using direct (agent-less) sales methods. Or they will shun the opportunity to leverage the massive amounts of new available data to make quicker and more informed decisions because the already successful business process works without it. Granted, the new methods would prove more efficient and meaningful than the existing processes, yet the organization is incapable of envisioning the new way because of their successes with the old way. In other words, Victory Disease and bureaucracy prevent growth in a viable organization because of its successful past.

Bureaucracy loves hierarchy. Left to its own devices, it embeds layers of leaders and employees in endless positions of restricted communications, leaving only certain people able to communicate with others depending on the hierarchical structure; meanwhile, messages are twisted and controlled as they travel up and down the bureaucratic chains of leadership. Each different authority level possesses their own monopoly on information and decisions. The more formal the bureaucracy, the more formidable the levels of approval. As bureaucracy becomes more formal and rigid, the more likely the presence of Victory Disease.

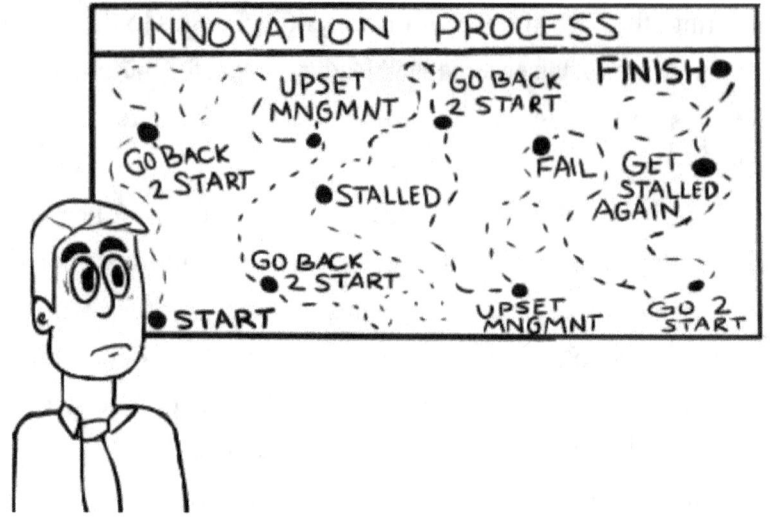

With budgets always caught up in the hierarchy, rules and the status quo determine expenditures more than good ideas. I recently worked with a bank CEO, supposedly the most powerful person in the organization, who felt he couldn't significantly influence his own organization's budget due to the many bureaucratic rules they had emplaced. As this example illustrates, bureaucracy essentially becomes a self-made and self-licking ice cream cone—building itself to support the organization, but then reinforcing the need to use that structure through excessive rules and monopolization of power. The result? The organization becomes so rigid and rules-driven that the organizational roles become subordinate to the bureaucracy. Meanwhile, the bureaucracy self-perpetuates itself through its own rules and processes, which stifle change and creativity. Taken another way, bureaucracy is to an organization what fat is to an individual. A certain amount of fat can prove necessary for your body to function normally, but excessive fat creates all kinds of problems, from heart disease to obesity. Likewise, bureaucracy remains essential for some processes, but excessive bureaucracy comprises a key component of Victory Disease and can easily strangle an organization's creative arteries.

CHAPTER 9
Bureaucracy in Action

Much like many successful, modern organizations, the Japanese operated as if they needed help from no one. Yet had they been willing to adjust and collaborate more with the Germans, their ally could have provided them benefits. While the Germans were employing valuable techniques that would have aided Japan's cause, the Japanese chose to operate independently, relying instead on their inherent right to victory.

One such partner opportunity was the chance to copy Germany's U-boat campaigns. The Germans were proving extremely successful in paralyzing Allied ship movement in the Atlantic, using submarines to sink the Allied logistics ships before they reached their destinations. Observing Japan's continued focus on sea dominance (believing it was their sea), numerous historians later noted the U-boat strategy would have flourished in the Japanese theater of operation. Yet the Japanese were unwilling to change their approach to traditional naval warfare to leverage this opportunity, preferring to continue with an outdated strategy. This frequent phenomenon occurring in business has become known as the "slow-follower" strategy, denoting when others don't follow quickly enough after a successful innovation emerges. Frequently bureaucracy is to blame since successful processes usually don't include avenues to find alternative processes or to disrupt themselves.

A Japanese Akutan Zero fighter

At the strategic level, the Japanese hierarchy was giving their people a lack of attention. They refused to listen to officers who espoused the creative use of air power and better methods of warfare, possibly their biggest oversight of the war. A large contingent of lower-ranking Japanese officers saw the shift in dominance from large ships to air power, but the hierarchical control of innovation from the top prevented a new air power strategy from materializing. In 1941, at the start of the war, the Japanese Zero fighters were better than any American plane. They could fly farther and perform better than any Allied aircraft, and their pilots had more fighter experience. But their old regime placed little emphasis on air power and never improved the Zero. Meanwhile, the Americans exploited air power innovation as fast as possible. American engines and radars were reinvented and improved. Old planes were upgraded, and other technologies were brought to bear. By 1944, just three years later, the Allies' planes and pilots proved notably superior.

The American Avenger, one of the surviving planes that was attacked while stationary at Pearl Harbor

Instead of embarking on the new aerial journey, the Japanese continued to build the same sort of battleships as before, only larger and less agile. The Japanese senior leadership committed to the existing doctrine that believed naval battles would comprise large, concentrated events that used bigger and bigger battleship guns to pound the enemy, with planes only useful to help identify enemy locations. Their doctrine proved sorely outdated as air power evolved into a force of its own. Unfortunately, the Japanese over-committed to the status quo by pouring huge sums of money and faith into the gigantic battleships, Musashi and Yamato. These expenditures illustrated incrementalism to the extreme.

The Musashi battleship

The Musashi under attack, just before sinking

These new, incredible Japanese sea vessels were the heaviest and most powerfully armed battleships ever constructed. They carried the largest naval artillery ever fitted to a warship: nine 18.1-inch naval guns, each capable of hurling 3,000-pound shells over twenty-six miles. If continuing the previous victorious ways was a winning formula, these battleships would have led the way. Yet as always the case with Victory Disease, alternative ideas remained unpursued, and Japanese airpower suffered. Instead, Japan emphasized the bigger and better ways of continuing the current models. After all, smaller battleships had secured previous triumphs, so producing bigger, more powerful battleships would, therefore, result in even larger victories.

Embodying the best of traditional thinking, the mammoth battleships were deployed against the innovative tactics of the U.S. military. Not surprisingly, the Americans' groundbreaking aerial and sub warfare soon saw success in countering the effectiveness of the old battleship mindset, shifting the tide of war to begin favoring America. The battlefield results began exposing the hierarchical bureaucracy of the Japanese Victory Disease.

As expected, incremental thinking lost to revolutionary thinking. Due to the threat of the more disruptive aircraft and subs, the mammoth Japanese battleships spent most of their time sitting in ports. When they were finally deployed, the results proved sadly predictable. U.S. aircraft bottomed the Musashi in 1944, and a submarine sank Yamato in 1945—fitting ends to the biggest, heaviest, and most armored battleships ever constructed. Japanese military analysts would later recognize them for what they really were—status-quo examples of Victory Disease.

Although impressive and unmatched, the new ships merely represented a larger version of an outdated model. Many young Japanese naval officers saw the need for more radical change, but their opinions went unheeded. The Japanese admirals created a culture incapable of envisioning anything other than incremental change and a continuation of their version of success. Many decision-makers could see evidence of global progress in aeronautical technology, aerial weapons, and aircraft, but Victory

Disease clouded their vision and prevented the military from acting on those changes. Meanwhile, the U.S. and Allies recognized the emerging importance of air power and initiated changes to capitalize on these burgeoning technologies and tactics. In fairness, the U.S. military actually benefited from the sudden damage and destruction to many of their battleships at Pearl Harbor as it forced them to look toward emerging technologies to boost their efforts.

Frequently, key organization leaders don't strongly identify Victory Disease symptoms until it's too late. With hindsight enhancing the diagnosis after the malady has pervaded and run amok, most notice it only after the organization's body has begun to atrophy. But by then it's often too late. If ignored, the disease metastasizes like an undetected cancer. The danger comes from how easily and gradually the symptoms can creep into the organizational fiber. Once Victory Disease has started to grow, stopping it proves challenging.

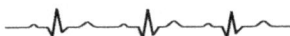

Practical Reflection: HIPPOs Are Extremely Dangerous

HIPPOs prove extremely dangerous and cause more deaths per year than some of the most feared animals in the world. Yes . . . HIPPOs. But rather than referring to the animal, I'm envisioning the Highest Paid Person's Opinion—*that* HIPPO. And these HIPPOs don't kill humans but rather slay new ideas and employee creativity. HIPPOs refer to the leaders in many organizations who always have an opinion concerning new ideas and innovations. And while HIPPOs supposedly climbed to their positions due to their tactical and managerial prowess, they are frequently the ones who will prematurely kill transformative solutions with a closed mindset. As the literal hippopotamus may attack humans to protect its domain, organizational HIPPOs think they are protecting the status quo from subordinates' crazy ideas. You can identify a HIPPO by their senior rank combined with an autocratic and risk-averse leadership style. This combination of traits makes the HIPPO lethal and one of the many unknown carriers of Victory Disease. The most lethal land animal is the hippopotamus, and the most dangerous organizational leader to new ideas is the HIPPO. Guard your young ideas closely and don't let them stray too close to a HIPPO.

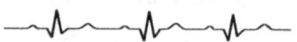

CHAPTER 10
Bureaucracy in Public Organizations

Public organizations are essentially prone to excessive bureaucracy—they remain bureaucratic at their core. But while not all bureaucracy is bad and some proves essential, unhealthy bureaucracy runs rampant in public organizations. Bad bureaucracy is bolstered by unnecessary processes, lack of customer focus, rigid policies, and hierarchy. Excessive bureaucracy strangles most forms of innovation and transformation, creating unbearable levels of approval and scrutiny that kill all but the most incremental and status quo ideas. A current example of bureaucracy supporting the status quo lies in the "boneyard" at Davis-Monthan Air Force Base in Arizona. The boneyard is home to about $35B (~4,500 planes) in unused aircraft—more than most countries' aircraft arsenal. This huge surplus of unwanted aircraft offers a testimony to the wastefulness of the large DoD bureaucracy. In 2013, the Air Force actually moved four brand-new C-27J Spartan aircraft from the production line directly to the boneyard, where fourteen others were already placed. Why? Because the bureaucratic hurdles made it easier to finish the aircraft and then immediately throw them away than to stop producing them. The Air Force spent a total of $527M dollars on the unwanted C-27Js. Bureaucracy at its worst results in wasted resources that support the status quo but could have driven innovation.

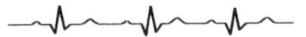

Practical Viewpoint: Lethal Bureaucracy in Public Organizations

Many public organizations appear terminally stricken with bureaucratic malaise. In 1969, the famous business writer Peter Drucker wrote his powerful article, "The Sickness of Government," in which he discusses the malaise of public organizations and their deep structural and systemic problems caused by excessive bureaucracy. And it's become much worse since then. The U.S. federal government spends trillions of dollars a year and is the number one driver of the huge U.S. federal deficit. Yet with all that money and resources, the public's satisfaction with federal services is lower than their satisfaction with private services in nearly every category. The underlying reason: excessive bureaucracy. After a lengthy study of the federal bureaucracy, Yale University law professor Peter Schuck concluded that "the public views the federal government as a chronically clumsy, ineffectual, bloated giant that cannot be counted upon to do the right thing, much less do it well."

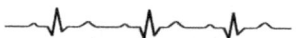

The private sector proves more effective at fighting bureaucracy than the public sector, but it still struggles. Many private organizations try to reduce bureaucracy by using lean processes and methods. They also try to lower the number of layers between leaders—flattening organizations and becoming leaner. The average number of executives reporting directly to corporate CEOs has increased substantially in recent decades while the number of organizational layers in Fortune 500 companies has fallen. Unfortunately, the typical public agency has increased its number of layers and titles. As an Army officer, I was acutely aware of the bureaucratic layering within the Department of Defense. It was terribly confusing to identify all the intermediary managers and political appointees in existence—the Assistant . . . to the Associate . . . to the Vice . . . to the Undersecretary . . . to the Deputy leaders, each with their own fiefdom and bureaucratically controlled area of influence. The more approval layers exist, the more innovation is stifled. Those who work at the Pentagon, the U.S. military headquarters, accurately call it the puzzle palace because of its mass bureaucratic confusion. Meanwhile in the marketplace, new ideas have no rank. They don't need rank, and they aren't made any better by the many complex layers of ranked people providing opinions.

Excessive bureaucracy in its many forms creates a rigid internal environment that basically shackles an organization's strides to innovate. Bureaucracy almost always perpetuates existing thinking and methods while erecting obstacles to the advancement of new ideas and innovative change—making it one of the three major symptoms of the dreaded Victory Disease.

CHAPTER 11

A Psychological Explanation for Bureaucracy—Bureaucrats Have Lost Their Minds

Modern psychologists have linked bureaucracies with the "theory of mind"—the ability to attribute mental states such as beliefs, intents, desires, emotions, and knowledge to one's own organization and to others. This cognitive ability also includes the understanding that others have beliefs, desires, intentions, and perspectives that are different from those of the organization. The theory of mind proves crucial for empathizing with customers and others outside the bureaucracy. Psychologists have rightly noted that people within a bureaucracy tend to lose their ability to empathize with others' thoughts and perspectives.

A theory of mind deficit is illustrated in an experiment exploring how a child lacks awareness of others. If you show a child a cracker box and ask "what's inside?" the child will reasonably guess "crackers." When the psychologist opens the box and shows the child the toys inside the cracker box, the child is surprised. Then the psychologist closes the cracker box with toys inside, and someone new enters the room. The psychologist asks the child what this new person believes is in the box. Now the child will say the new person will know that toys are inside as the child has inadequate ability to discern that the new person doesn't have their same understanding or viewpoint. When the psychologist tells the child that the new person hasn't seen the surprise in the box, it doesn't matter to the child because the child can't discern the difference. The theory of mind shows us that children up to a certain age (and some impaired adults) have a deficiency in the ability to know that others don't have their same understanding or beliefs.

This lack of mindful ability occurs within bureaucracies and the people that operate within them as well. The bureaucrats (like the child in the example) wield their knowledge as if it were everyone's knowledge. They have theory of mind failures because they know that their bureaucracy works and, therefore, they don't have to recognize anything outside their accepted bureaucratic process. The organization heavily burdened with bureaucracies propagates the failure to recognize others' beliefs, so new ideas that fail to fit into existing beliefs are pushed aside, not recognized, or even killed. Bureaucrats haven't really lost their minds, just their ability to realize that other opinions besides theirs are valid.

The "C" of Victory Disease:
Complacency

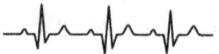

Complacency is the last hurdle standing between
any team and its potential greatness.
                                        —Pat Riley

CHAPTER 12
Complacency Defined

Complacency marks the third and final symptom of Victory Disease. I refer to it as the *quiet killer* because complacency is the morphine death of organizations—a quiet, comfortable way to drift into irrelevance that many successful organizations experience. The symptom manifests through an organization's unawareness of the dangers and threats to their business model, usually characterized by a calm contentment with their position and lack of desire to disrupt their comfortable environment. Complacent organizations lose their competitive edge because they aren't challenging themselves anymore. Mediocrity is accepted and becomes the norm, and with fear of failure always around the corner, the complacent organization prefers not to take any chances.

In today's hyper-innovation environment, an organization must consciously choose to act complacent. It's not something that just happens unaware. Too many leaders, employees, and partners exist who are more than willing to share information about emerging trends and concepts. One merely needs to listen. Yet in a company with Victory Disease symptoms, those alternative voices are silenced and not provided an organizational outlet. The alternative voices speak up, but the culture shuts them down. As mentioned previously, many of those who speak up are branded as troublemakers for even mentioning or suggesting alternative trends or innovations. Eventually, the perceived troublemakers are either silenced or leave the company for somewhere more proactive, and the complacent organization continues on with the status quo reigning supreme.

In my line of financial services, complacency is almost always tied to leadership. The leadership in the big financial services companies hold very nice positions, making large salaries and running well-oiled businesses. They're multi-millionaires who have climbed the ladder to obtain their success. Very few want to rock the boat with change or disruptive ideas as their seat in the boat might be threatened. They never want others to view them as troublemakers, or worse, as disruptors to the status quo. Therefore, they patiently manage the status quo and fend off big change that could risk their position. After all, they have just a few years left until they will achieve their personal wealth goals, and that aim is what motivates most of them. The status quo thrives in organizations where leadership sits complacent. Status quo thinking causes them to lose market share, business, and customers while they manage it all from the comfort of large offices and comfy board rooms. Complacent organizations lose consciousness about the outside world and ignore the transformative advances happening in their market.

CHAPTER 13

Japanese Complacency

Like many of today's successful organizations, the Japanese enjoyed a long history of past success. Many of the Japanese leaders operated with a level of naïve satisfaction and ignorance that encouraged complacency—so much so that complacency became the standard. But how did they so quickly become complacent and lose their competitive edge?

As a very homogeneous warrior-class, the Japanese felt like their history and genetics gave them a natural upper-hand in the art of war. From the effective defense of Japan against the powerful Mongols in the 13th century, to the defeat of tsarist Russia in the early 20th century, the Japanese proved their military prowess repeatedly. Their proud heritage was one of victory and conquest, so they treated victory as the natural state of affairs. In fact, Japan wouldn't have even existed without the historical success of its warrior class.

In World War II, when brave Japanese challengers to the status quo spoke up, they were frequently reminded of the history of Japanese dominance and the Pearl Harbor successes. During the war's early stages, the Japanese held victory parties that illustrated their complacency and arrogance. During these parties (whether they won or not), they reinforced their victories to each other and encouraged the belief that success would continue, no matter what happened.

Across the officer ranks, they toasted each other with congratulations and praise: "Long live the Emperor and Japanese victory!" They reveled in their triumphs and discounted the initial ingenuity that got them there. Their victory parties entailed external confirmations to each other that they were winning and were winners. The concept of losing and failure almost became obsolete in their culture. A young officer's journal recalls that, during the celebrations, they would sit cross-legged around a large table and celebrate until succumbing to food and alcohol comas. As the replenishing of drinks symbolized their continued success, they would customarily refill each other's glasses for hours on end. The much-used drinking toast, "To Japanese superiority," first began at these parties and continued throughout the war.

After large parties ended for the night, most of the Japanese officers would split into smaller groups and continue the celebration at more informal parties with other officers and, sometimes, geisha girls. The victory parties were frequent enough to fill the officer corps with a strong sense of their glorious wins. One officer's journal read, "I work and I nomikai (the Japanese term for *victory party*), with no time for sleep."

But victory parties don't win future engagements. By believing no military changes were necessary, they failed to listen to the environment or invest in strategic innovations. They celebrated victory as if the innovation component was insignificant, thus cementing their belief in an inherent right to victory. Complacency didn't allow the study or full understanding of the environment or the threats. They did not analyze them completely as they had no desire to do so. In Japan, this led to incomplete or ill-advised battle plans—and to good soldiers dying due to half-baked strategies.

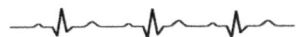

Practical Reflection: The Extravagances of Success

In many successful U.S. organizations, the executives also celebrate their successes with extravagant parties, rich food, and expensive entertainment. Although different from Japanese victory parties, they share some of the same components. Like infectious agents, these events propagate a false sense of organizational entitlement.

Tyco, the large successful U.S. security firm, is noted for holding large and excessive celebration parties. At the height of their success, their infamous CEO paid a reported $2M of company money for his wife's birthday party. The party was held on the Italian island of Sardinia and featured an ice sculpture of Michelangelo's David urinating Stolichnaya vodka. The celebration included a private concert by Jimmy Buffett. The shareholder meetings shared similar extravagant features. These lavish events were later branded as "Tyco Roman Orgies" after the company went public about them and decided to correct the arrogant behavior of their senior leaders. The CEO was ultimately convicted of stealing $150M from Tyco and served jail time for some of his antics.

Excessive parties are, of course, celebrations, and who doesn't like a party? But they also serve to propagate the belief that success will continue to happen inevitably. Extravagance in organizations unknowingly creates internal vulnerabilities when their leaders don't invest any of that celebratory spirit to develop more innovation.

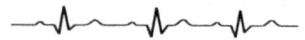

CHAPTER 14

Complacency in Action

Even though the dangers of the status quo are easy to see, many of today's market leaders operate under covert complacency. They prefer to remain unaware of the need for long-term innovations and, instead, focus on short-term gains and quarterly earnings, believing that things will continue as before. Yet, complacent leaders will always have nice things to say about innovation. After all, it's one of the biggest buzzwords in modern day business. So, they openly support it in their public statements and may even have a few innovation books in their bookcase behind their desk. But that's where the support stops. Covertly, they know they will take none of the risks required to make innovation successful, and therefore, don't spend their own time on it nor allocate resources.

Covert complacency proves hard to detect, but because I'm allowed into the inner workings of the senior leadership teams, I see it all the time. In my interview protocol, I ask a series of questions to senior leaders to determine their real capacity for change. First, I ask them what *innovation* means to them and how they feel about organizational change. This question evokes a 100 percent approval rating for innovation, often accompanied with amazing stories of change (with Steve Jobs frequently mentioned). But then I ask the follow up question, "If someone were to find an innovative solution to your problems that you can't currently solve, would you support it with resources?" This illustrates where their complacency come to light as most of leaders who praised innovation are now forced to consider a very real resource-commitment question. Over 90 percent of them will hem and haw about their shrinking budget, commitments made already, and many other excuses. They say they really love innovation, but somehow haven't resourced any and just can't find a way to do so.

Complacent leaders sit atop many successful organizations because success naturally breeds a sense of security. They become so content with their big paychecks and bonuses earned from previous product and service initiatives that they lose their competitive edge and allow upstarts to steal their market share. In my field of financial services, it's a multi-millionaires' club reclining at the top of the leadership chains, with large bonuses and golden parachutes that make the concept of long-term success easily forgotten. Leaders of successful organizations are (for the most part) smugly happy with their current leadership and success, making it difficult to root out complacency. Many senior leaders will use efficiency and discipline to suck the life from their organizations, never take any real risks, and never care that their behavior is part of the malaise hurting the organization. Complacency is one of the most well-hidden enemies of innovation because it's usually detected only by seeing what an organization *isn't* doing.

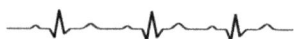

Practical Viewpoint:
Research in Motion—Research Without Motion
    Research in Motion, or RIM, was the company that once owned the world's most recognizable gadget, the BlackBerry. That wonderful handheld device was a marvelous invention that propelled RIM to a market valuation of more than $80B and inspired users everywhere to acknowledge their dependence on the device. I, too, was a "crackberry" addict, using the device as a transformation officer within the DoD and seeing its power as we rebuilt the hurricane-torn New Orleans back to health. As the transformation officer assigned to the New Orleans mayor's office, I was not surprised to find their operations, as well as those of the U.S. military response, dependent on the

BlackBerrys for the most reliable communications. The BlackBerry company, RIM, soared to an all-time high while I was assisting New Orleans with the rebuild, and we loved its product. But RIM leaders became so mired in complacency that they allowed their dominant position to dwindle to nothing.

A myriad of business articles out there analyze the reasons for the RIM demise, including the rise of the iPhone, a shift to software over hardware solutions, and a fractured leadership structure—all of which are valid. But if you examine the root cause of their death, it was related to their success and not wanting to deviate from it. All their ailments stemmed from a stolid feeling of contentment, not possessing an urgency to change. RIM had pioneered the wireless email market and became a dominant force in the early 2000s, but then essentially sat on the sidelines and watched as iPhone and Android invented options that grew to seize the market. The root cause was mired in complacency. BlackBerry owned the market and could have moved in any direction it wanted. But their company, Research in Motion, was guilty of research *without* motion. They chose to ignore the new entrants and emphasis on apps, and instead used an incremental approach to simply make small changes to what was already working. Like the Japanese in WWII choosing to build bigger and better battleships (and ignore air power), so RIM chose to merely improve their platform and ignore the emergence of disruptive changes such as apps and software. Co-CEO Jim Balsillie in 2007 stated, "It's okay—we'll be fine." Complacency caused RIM and the BlackBerry to rapidly decline. Now that Victory Disease has taken its course, the company has finally committed to change, but it came at huge cost with only a small bit of market share left— and even less resources to make significant changes.

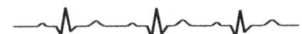

CHAPTER 15

Cognitive Dissonance—A Psychological Explanation for Complacency

Cognitive dissonance is the modern term for the uncomfortable feeling we have when we are confronted with two conflicting beliefs, or dissonance. Modern social scientists have declared cognitive dissonance as a powerful influence on our behavior because we naturally try to reduce or resolve the conflict. Cognitive dissonance occurs in many areas of life but is especially evident in places where complacency exists. So, while I like to hold leaders in contempt for their complacency, some psychological reasons (besides lack of personal courage) add to its prevalence.

Dissonance in the business arena illustrates a classic conflict between transforming and running the organization. The conflict arises between uncertainty and certainty, stress and no stress. In the case of complacency and Victory Disease, the conflict works like this:

- Innovations and transformations are occurring that I want to be part of, BUT
- It's important for me to continue running the business the same way because I've been successful.

Transforming the organization involves radical change and often disintermediates elements of the business while *running the business* allows smooth and steady management, with any changes deemed incremental and not radical. Ideally, leaders can both transform and run the business, but that currently marks the exception and not the rule. Some modern theorists have coined the term *ambidextrous*[6] to describe the ideal posture of organizational leaders who can do both. They can both transform and run the business simultaneously. On the one hand, they can continue the organization's current success, and on the other hand they are able to reinvent the organization through new solutions. But as ambidextrous people prove rare in the physical world, so they prove rare in organizations. This fact leaves most leaders in cognitive dissonance over what to do.

When faced with the dissonance between transforming and running the business, most leaders play it safe and run the business.

They almost always justify their decision to focus on running the business with a common set of excuses. Attached is a word picture of leader excuses that I started writing down while I was leading a large innovation program. I call it an "organization's last words."

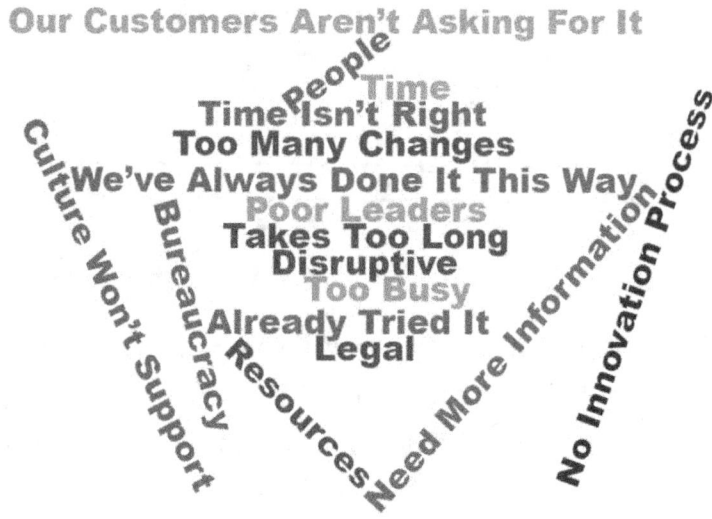

An Organization's Last Words

Now as a consultant, I continue to hear the same set of common excuses. In my market of financial services, risk excuses always rise to the top. Reasons such as "the risk is too high" and "ROI isn't predictable" are frequently espoused. The best ideas in the organization are reduced to the point of not being good ideas anymore, or they're flat-out ignored. And when it comes to funding decisions, the risk-averse leaders will always select the less risky (lower reward) projects with predictable paths over the riskier (higher reward) projects that are less predictable. The non-innovative leaders then reduce their cognitive dissonance by downplaying the transformative ideas as being too risky, or not right for the organization. As a first-hand witness to these behaviors, I can attest that risk-averse leaders have a habit of eliminating risk and then convincing themselves that they made the right decision.

Dying organizations are full of people who have ignored or killed transformational opportunities in favor of the more conservative business options. While I focus on the leaders as they have the most opportunity, it happens at all levels of the organization. While leading programs on my innovation journey, I coined the term "frozen middle" to refer to the mid-level employees who can slow or kill ideas. Complacency manifests itself in the overworked managers who don't have time to take chances and in the project managers who don't want to risk failure. They delay and kill ideas because they perceive it's in their best interest to do so. Their complacency features strong psychological underpinnings. In most cases, employees and leaders of Victory Diseased organizations cannot become ambidextrous, so they must rationalize away the reasons they are not transforming the business. Their cognitive dissonance drives them to complacency. And, similar to the Japanese during World War II, they usually find a way to comfortably rationalize their complacency.

The Signs and Symptoms
of the Disease

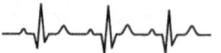

"It's easy to come up with new ideas; the hard part
is letting go of what worked for you two years
ago, but will soon be out of date."
—Roger von Oech

CHAPTER 16

The Compound Effect of the ABCs

The danger of Victory Disease comes from how easily it infects a successful organization. Big or small, private or public, an organization often becomes symptomatic of Victory Disease wherever success has occurred. And while any one of the symptoms proves dangerous, when all three infect an organization at the same time, a terminal prognosis can result.

The combination of arrogance, bureaucracy, and complacency becomes a powerful force against any innovation. If all three are present, problems in the organization will surface everywhere but will be ignored or downplayed. For all three to exist means that every part of the organization languishes in denial. Much like the Japanese in World War II, the infected entity is quickly atrophying towards death.

At the employee level, that means employees aren't going above and beyond to do anything besides their basic job requirements, and, you guessed it—they're not even doing those well. They often hide themselves behind bureaucracy to earn a paycheck and have no accountability for the organization's well-being. At the management level, the so-called leaders serve as order takers who explicitly follow rules and do nothing beyond the scope of their assigned functions. The managers might even make up work to look busy or fall into routines of mediocrity, where the status quo is preferred. And at the senior leader level? They are counting money and ignoring reality. In other words, no one is really trying. Victory Disease symptoms dampen the ability of all affected participants to make a difference, when a difference is sorely needed.

Print media illustrates one such group with all three symptoms of Victory Disease. For years, print media set the agenda for what news we see and how we see it. In the past, trusted reporters and their news outlets, including *The New York Times*, *Chicago Tribune*, and *TIME* magazine, became trusted household fixtures for much of America.

But for the past several years their market has seen steady decline. All the big publishers are immersed in the process of closing or consolidating titles; print news audiences are continuously dwindling; and daily newspaper reading has been free-falling for years. We are witnessing the painful demise of mainstream media. As more and more readers are getting their news from other sources across the Internet, the mainstream media has proved largely incapable of reinventing itself in the digital age, exhibiting all the symptoms of Victory Disease.

We are witnessing the old standards quickly becoming obsolete as Victory Disease symptoms have corrupted the once dominant market. In essence, the convergence of information and distribution channels has created a wonderland of information, an amazing environment that gives each of us the ability to be a reporter, a publisher, an on-scene photographer. And although print media at one time was well-positioned to capitalize on the new paradigm, they failed to act—opting instead for the status quo, even as their market and customer preferences transformed. Now the market no longer wants a packaged solution proffered as the news, a boxed emulsion that a handful of media moguls sitting in a New York building has decided to feed us. Yet, that's mostly the model they're still trying to sell.

In this print media market, arrogance prevails. Yes, those same media moguls who previously dominated have mostly ignored the signs of the coming changes. Because they believe they set the agenda for what the public consumes and believes, their arrogance is a powerful aphrodisiac that they don't seem capable of overcoming. Even amidst falling ratings, sexual harassment scandals, and public distrust at all-time highs, most of the mass media is still happy to plod along with their old business model, ignoring the stench of death within their organizations. In print media, it's not that it's unrecognizable; everyone finally sees it. It's that they can't transform their business model. They don't want to give up their positions of power. They almost seem more willing to commit their businesses to die rather than accept change. It's akin to the Japanese officers in World War II who chose to commit ritualistic suicide rather than acknowledge their mistakes and improve. The arrogance of wanting to stay in ignorance loomed so powerful that many Japanese officers committed ritual suicide.

Now, major mass media organizations are also on a path to painful public deaths. Their arrogance appears persistent to the bitter end. They completely missed the democratization of the news, believing they could set the agenda forever even as online independent voices became stronger. What's worse, many of their customers believe they have lost the ability to maintain objectivity in providing the facts. The arrogance of the high-paid mainstream media's newscasters and editors has created the worst all-time trust figures in the last seventy-five years. A 2016 Gallup poll showed confidence in the media had fallen to an all-time low. Again, in 2018, the *Axios* news website was noting, "New poll shows trust in the media at an all-time low on both sides of the aisle." Now with public confidence in mainstream media in steady decline— signaling a glaring loss of trust in their journalistic objectivity— people are largely getting their news from other sources. The trifecta of Victory Disease components has mega-media giants like *TIME* magazine rapidly losing revenue and market share. With a steadily declining market, diminished circulation, and less advertising revenue, *TIME* clings precariously on the Victory Disease slippery slope.

TIME Person of the Year cover for themselves (journalists)

What should you do if you're *TIME* magazine, the once lofty leader of mass media, stumbling in serious decline? Well, you merely ignore the truth (or at least the public's perception of it) and declare journalists the current saviors of the world. Much like the Japanese officers who attended elaborate parties on account of their previous victories (while ignoring their Victory Disease), so too the declining mainstream press decided to celebrate itself with accolades, awards, and exclusive press clubs. In fact, *TIME* magazine decided to name journalists, yes, *themselves*, as the 2018 "Person of the Year." They called the journalists "guardians."

This attitude smacks amazingly similar to the Japanese

leaders who rewarded themselves as their war efforts died under the plunder of previous success. For those in the media today, their professions as they know them are rapidly dying as they slide off the mountain of self-congratulatory overload. I'm not suggesting that some (or even many) journalists aren't maintaining journalistic integrity. But to name themselves "Person of the Year" while their customers have left in droves because they doubt the media's integrity is just being tone-deaf to an unreasonable degree. Like the Japanese leadership of World War II, it's as if they believe they have the power to change reality by merely imposing their skewed beliefs on the public. As with the Japanese, it will work with those insiders who want to believe, but for the rest of the world based more in reality, it will fall flat. Nomikai victory parties and patting yourself on the back doesn't win future battles, and giving yourself awards for journalistic integrity doesn't mean you actually have it or that you can regain the customers' trust you've lost. Accolades and rewards are representations of success, but because they really mask illness they are just a false diagnosis of health. The underlying malady still exists causing even more damage to the organization that is in denial.

Bureaucracy, which can be a good thing, now blockades the way of traditional media. Their large, bloated departments are staffed by people who specialize in specific areas: printing, technology, sports, etc. Contrast that with their competition, the new market entrants, who care not about organizational structure but about dispersing the right content. Certainly, print media made printing a science, with major newspapers cranking out the latest and greatest information twice daily. Print media became masters of time and distribution. But digitization changed all that.

IT'S INFECTING EVERYTHING!

Much like the film company Eastman Kodak perfected film processing in the 20th century, so newspapers and publishers perfected printing. The game changed for them both, however, to digital content, available anytime and anywhere the customer wants it. Because they refined and perfected their printing trade till it reached the pinnacle of possible efficacy, they were reluctant to cast off the bureaucracy of their victorious processes. For decades, newspapers gathered the very best information and analysis within a 24-hour period, magically delivering it to your doorstep rain or shine. The gears that made it work didn't see themselves ever supplanted by something simpler and less cumbersome— something not subject to the bureaucracy of deadlines and processes. Online media has usurped the efficiency of print media without even trying. Digital information is available anytime and anywhere, unencumbered by the bureaucracy of a printing press or a hierarchical approval process of an editorial group. It simply reports.

The very efficiencies of print media are disrupted as the entrenched bureaucracies that once dominated are now forced to undergo budget and personnel cuts as their market dwindles. They were sadly in the best position to capitalize on the new business model, but twenty years of complacency have now led them to what appears as total disruption of their business. Advertisers are rapidly moving online and to alternative platforms, profits are plunging, print is way down, and yet . . . the mainstream media stays in denial. Their traditional funding model is drying up, with advertisers pursuing newer, more effective business models. And what has happened to the once mighty *TIME* magazine discussed above? After purchasing it late in 2018, a billionaire software company CEO doesn't appear to care that it's dying and is ironically reported to have purchased it as a "platform of change."[7]

The malaise of news organizations is tied in many ways to the entire mass media business model. Mainstream broadcasting, printing, book publishing—it's all dying before our eyes. The mainstream press is atrophying because it has succumbed to every symptom of Victory Disease: arrogance, bureaucracy, and complacency. And the disease doesn't appear limited to American media; everywhere, mainstream media languishes in decline and distrust, with online sources grabbing larger and larger shares. Once the colossal media giants owned the market share and sat in the perfect position to capitalize on the new way of delivering content, but the compounding effect of Victory Disease is ruthlessly overcoming them, and we're witnessing their decline.

CHAPTER 17
Innovate or Die

Pick a market, any market, and if you look hard enough you'll see some elements of Victory Disease. Many of today's organizations are struggling with its ravaging effects while a rare few are overcoming or averting them to establish market dominance. A recent Washington University study projected that nearly half of today's Fortune 500 companies on the S&P 500 index will cease to exist in 10 years,[8] a record-breaking pace of diminishment. Yet CEO compensation has grown 940% since 1978.[9] The climate has never been more conducive for Victory Disease.

Monumental shifts are occurring in the world, happening in every market and social strata. The rapid advances in technology and digital data are revolutionizing the way we live and conduct business. Whether in private sectors, public sectors, advanced societies, basic societies, change is everywhere. Successful companies must learn to adapt, or they will die. The products and services currently making them successful will prove inadequate for the near future of disruptive technologies, shifting markets, and changing public demand. While later in this book I provide some proven solutions for organizations willing to adapt, the very first thing they must do is recognize that change is necessary. If organizations don't become conscious of the constant need for change and adapt their approaches accordingly, they will perish.

The essential time for a successful organization to embrace change is while at the top. From the top, they have the market share and capital to try new approaches and venture into innovative solutions. Yet it's very hard for a successful organization to realize that need. Usually, the people who call for change during good times are marginalized and seen as troublemakers. Why change when everything is going so well? Why make waves? Leaders who ignore the disease love to say, "If it ain't broke, don't fix it." And when troubled times surface for the successful organization (perhaps their earnings are down, or their market growth has slowed), they usually try to get back to the original ideas and ways that made them successful. Not realizing the rapidity of the change occurring elsewhere, they reinforce their old business models.

That's when Victory Disease infests the organization; its leaders silence or eliminate the change agents as the cause of the problem, and thus reinforce the status quo. But when the status quo doesn't work, no matter how hard they try to reinforce it, someone finally recognizes the need for change. But often it's too late.

The life of great organizations proves a lot like the life of great people. They can, and do, end abruptly. The health and wellness of an organization's future is directly related to how well they adapt and influence change. Some will learn to recognize and adapt quickly while many will fail to adapt and die. Following is a closer look at three organizations that are in rapid decline from Victory Disease: a public organization (the U.S. Postal Service), a mixed private and public industry (higher education), and a private industry (taxicabs).

CHAPTER 18

Sick Public Organization: The United States Postal Service

Private organizations aren't the only victims of Victory Disease; it affects all organizations, public and private. One such public organization currently in its throes is the U.S. Postal Service. With a storied history, the great and mighty post office is unfortunately teetering on the brink of insolvency. Neither snow, rain, heat, nor gloom of night can stop the postal service, but Victory Disease definitely can.

The recent history of the USPS has been one mired in bureaucracy. With the rise of the Internet eliminating much of the need for first-class mail, the postal service doesn't appear able to get out of its own way and do something else as it slowly chugs towards obsolescence. First-class mail, its number one revenue earner, has been rapidly replaced with emails and online communications. First-class mail has been cut into a fraction of its former self in the last twenty years, from about sixty billion pieces in 1996 to less than twenty billion today. Digital mail has become central to long-distance communications while the USPS has remained on the sidelines, watching.

The postal service had a front row seat to see it all happening but was too encumbered by the weight of their own bureaucracy to do much about it. Their 503,000 employees and 30,825 managed retail offices[10] remained virtually unchanged as their main line of business was radically influenced by market innovations such as online bill pay and apps that streamline communications. What's possibly worse lies in the reality that they've allowed themselves to become the leader of what most of us now consider junk mail, or standard mail. Comprised of advertisements, political messages, and unrequested solicitations, this standard mail seems to jam up and take over our postal boxes weekly. By doing nothing to reform their mail operations, the USPS has allowed a formerly premium customer experience to become a depressing one.

One of my recent business trips illustrates the precarious position where the postal service finds itself. I typically schedule my travel weeks to occur Monday through Friday so I'm home on the weekends. During a recent weekly travel trip, my home mailbox became overstuffed with second class mail (i.e., junk mail). Keep in mind, I was only gone five days. So, seeing a mailbox overstuffed with junk mail, my mail carrier stopped my service and held all my mail at the main post office. Upon my return, I was forced to go to the post office to reopen my box and was greeted by a forty-five-minute line to wait my turn. Upon turning "on" my box and sifting through my mail, I discovered it was comprised of thirty-seven parcels of trash and just two useful letters. As I threw the junk mail in the post office trash, I did the math on how much waste the postal service and junk mailers were causing.

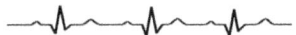

Personal Reflection: The Costs of Postal Service Victory Disease
 Tree deaths: 37 pieces of junk mail per week X 52 weeks X 100 million American households = 192.4 billion parcels of junk each year. Assuming that one tree is able to supply 8,000 junk mailings, their junk mail service is annually costing the environment about 24 million trees.
 Time wasted: Assuming 10 seconds per junk parcel using the same numbers above, total time wasted equals about 52 hours per household per year. Or more than a work week per household is annually wasted on junk mail.

I used to like the postal service and can fondly remember waiting as a child for a treasured magazine or Christmas card from Grandma in the mail—but making memories like this is quickly becoming archaic. For most people, magazines have become extinct and Grandma is on Facebook. For me, I can only describe the recent customer experiences as painful. I hate standing in lines, dislike wasting my time screening junk mail, and detest wasting paper. One of my most unhappy moments in my routine is checking my mail. Yet, that is the experience the USPS is now delivering to me and many others.

As is often the case with organizations riddled with Victory Disease, the once great products of the postal service have become irritations; not just their mail service, but some of its differentiating features that once made it special are now obsolete nuisances. The ZIP code, an incredible innovation from the 1960s, now has four more digits dangling on its end that no one really understands or cares about. The ZIP code, short for "zone improvement plan" code, was an improved way to deliver packages, with the code's five digits representing the destination's region and locale. It proved a phenomenal success, so in the '80s the postal service decided to make it even more granular by adding four more digits, making it the ZIP+4. However, it didn't catch on; people were annoyed by having to remember additional esoteric details, and most importantly, new innovations made it unnecessary. Yet those four extra digits were embraced by the clueless federal bureaucracy and now cause more confusion and waste even more time. Technology-enabled automatic mail sorting systems eliminated the need for people to use the +4 numbers. Like the Japanese in World War II creating a bigger battleship, even though air power technology was coming into force, so too the U.S. Postal Service continued with their ZIP numbering. The bureaucracy wrongly reasoned that if five digits were good, then nine digits would be even better. Yet as the postal service launched the extra numbers to an unhappy customer, the technology was ready to deploy optical readers to sort mail without forcing the customer to do more.

If their product line demise wasn't bad enough, the USPS has a failing business model and needs radical innovation ASAP. Like a cancer that starts small and grows to infect larger organs and tissues, with the whole body structure eventually affected, so their product demise and innovation infirmities have spread to their entire business structure. Salaries and benefits now make up a whopping ~80 percent of their budget, which in some cases are double what United Parcel or FedEx pay.[11] And . . . their retirements and benefits costs are out of control, thanks to some of the highest paid semi-skilled workers in the world. Why? For years they have placed the interests of their unions first, allowing personnel costs to skyrocket without the requisite income to match the raises.

Quality leadership is a key to recognizing and overcoming Victory Disease, yet unfortunately the U.S. Congress resides in the leadership chain of the USPS. Congress has a hand in this diseased organization and must get out of the postal service's way or quickly provide the leadership it needs to heal. This inopportune union has produced a discombobulated set of operating policies with very little innovation. Congress tells them to act more like a business but subsequently hamstrings them from making smart business decisions. While supposedly entirely independent of government funding with taxpayer dollars, the USPS must still endure Congress' constant micromanagement. For example, if the USPS desires to close an unprofitable post office, Congress can intervene and prevent the closure. Congress micromanages them through by-laws and regulations, exemplifying that far too much bureaucracy exists to overcome a serious case of Victory Disease.

Although the postal service was admired and respected (and even has a place in the U.S. Constitution), the symptoms of Victory Disease are destroying this once-great organization. The previously respected and revered postal service is dying and doesn't seem able to cut through the bureaucracy to administer an antidote.

CHAPTER 19

Feverish Public/Private Victim: Higher Education

As a seasoned Board member for innovation at two higher education institutions, I see strong elements of Victory Disease everywhere within higher ed. If one looks at the environment in higher education, it is drastically changing. The proliferation of online information has been nothing short of remarkable. Everything . . . *every*thing is available online. Yet most higher education classrooms seem fixated on physical space and in-person interactions with a professor talking from a platform. The primary customers, the students, are continually online for other pursuits. They expect information immediately when they want it, when they need it, and how they need it. The concept of set times and schedules is anathema to them. Yet traditional higher education systems insist on their old in-person prescription for education.

Society, the major customer of higher education, is begging for more science, technology engineering, and math (STEM) skilled employees. The United States is woefully short of STEM qualified workers, yet the education system isn't responding quickly to their needs.

Meanwhile, many professors arrogantly resist change, insisting on teaching their way, with each classroom serving as a mini fiefdom that they control. It reminds me of the separate industry lines within the business world in which leaders feel both responsibility and ownership for their businesses but use that separateness to shut down innovation. Likewise, professors own the classrooms and often refuse outside influences.

The bureaucracy of most higher education institutions wraps

itself around forward progress in onerous ways. And in doing so, really prevents new ideas from growing. Just the concept of tenured professors inhibits change and drastically reduces accountability for classroom delivery and content. There is a proliferation of tenured professors who see themselves as irreplaceable sages, with 20-page syllabi and pompous attitudes. They represent the samurai of the education system, doling out the same old topics using archaic and outdated methods. Why? Because they've always done it that way.

Meanwhile, their customers are gaining so much student loan debt that it has become a national crisis. Students are forced to spend money they don't have, for courses they don't want, delivered in a manner they don't prefer. The average student now graduates with greater than $30K of student loans, a massive amount of burden for new job entrants to bear.

To get a taste of the massive bureaucratic structures that represent traditional higher education, try to navigate any one of their websites. You will quickly become overwhelmed with categories . . . and specialties . . . and processes . . . and organizations . . . and bureaucracy. And it's even worse to visit the campus to try to figure out where to go. Victory Disease is everywhere on campus.

CHAPTER 20
Private Organization: The Taxi Industry

The taxicab business illustrates an entire industry in the latter stages of Victory Disease— although many within its own ranks don't recognize the phenomenon (confirming it really is in dire straits). Although not as vaunted as those in postal delivery, taxicab drivers have joined a profession with a long and successful history. The modern taxi, a term taken from the word *taxes*, meaning tax or levy, has existed since the advent of the automobile. Taxi drivers and their company employers have owned the short-distance people-transport business for most of the twentieth century. Since the early 1900s, they've enjoyed dominating the city customer transport business and dictating the experience, proving extremely successful at this endeavor.

Taxi company business models are intertwined with city ordinances and regulations to control and select the exact number of taxi licenses to serve their communities. Taxi licenses, sometimes called medallions, are a tradeable commodity and once yielded high dollars based on their expected revenue generation. Previously, medallions not only increased in value, they also produced a steady income stream for the owner, who assigned them to a car for daily usage. Different models then evolved for the actual taxi drivers, whereby some could own their own medallions and some merely rented the right to use the taxi company's medallions. The model worked marvelously well, with taxis profitably operating as a virtual monopoly in many large cities. However, the model was predicated on owning the experience with no competition.

The advent of ride-sharing services such as Uber and Lyft

changed the business model and potential customer experience drastically. Ridesharing allows new market entrants to transport customers more quickly and efficiently than the taxi-cab model. Where the taxi model forces potential customers to compete on street corners where customers essentially beg overworked cabs to pick them up, the ride-sharing model allows an orderly and scheduled pickup at the time and place of the customer's choice. Ridesharing offers a superior customer experience.

The influx of ridesharing has halted the growth of traditional taxi business models and sent them into a spiraling descent of perceived value. The previously lucrative taxi medallions are now tanking and becoming horrible investments. Once going for a million-plus dollars in NYC, taxi medallions now cost less than half of that. Meanwhile, bureaucracy—the horrible Victory Disease symptom—is alive and well in the taxi battle culture.

Instead of transforming, taxicab companies are arguing that cities and municipalities need more regulation on the ride-sharing services, protesting that the taxi service option needs bureaucracy for "the other guy"—in Uber and Lyft—to make taxis relevant again. More bureaucracy, in the form of regulations and rules, is contrary to the improved customer experience that ride-sharing brings. Most times that an organization argues for more bureaucracy, it signals a losing proposition, as is evident in this case. It's like a lung cancer patient arguing for more cigarettes; it will make them feel better for the moment but will ultimately result in more sickness. We are currently witnessing taxicab unions and companies protesting to their municipalities to make their unholy alliance stronger through more laws and regulations on ridesharing. But they are arguing against the customer experience. They are arguing against innovation and progress.

Taxi drivers were at one time the samurais of their driving profession. They were the hands-down experts on traffic flow, knowing which routes were best and worst at what times. In the U.S., experienced cab drivers were valuable human maps, possessing the optimal information about navigating roads in record times. And in some cities like London, taxi drivers' professional knowledge grew even more impressive as intensive training required on the nuances of routes and causeways earned them a "green" badge.

But thanks to various innovations including GPS, cab drivers' expertise, no matter how skilled, is becoming irrelevant. Now, map programs and applications can select the best route with no memorization needed. Coveted green badges in London have been replaced by simple technology. Updated traffic patterns can be viewed in real-time on any smart phone. Pickup and drop-off points are scheduled to the nearest minute and meter while providing identifying information to the travelers and driver. If a customer wants to be picked up at 1 Wall Street at 11:59 a.m. in a four-door SUV, three clicks on an app can get it done. Not only is the process precise, but both the customer and ride-share driver can confirm the transaction in advance. No guessing or transaction mystery are involved, delivering a "wow!" customer experience that proficiently drives demand.

Given all these fantastic transportation innovations, one would expect taxi companies to follow suit with their own radical changes. But that's not the case. Taxi drivers—the samurais of the road—still consider themselves the masters of the people-transport business, even though their knowledge has become less relevant and at times even outdated. Their map and route knowledge is inferior to any digital app, yet most refuse to use GPS-type technology. Their traffic knowledge has become old and stale compared to the real-time updates available, yet they refuse to consult traffic apps. And their model of telling the customer what route options are best for them instead of consulting and involving the customer results in frustrated people stuck in traffic or higher fee situations who know better routes were available. A recent taxi study reported that ride-sharing significantly undercut the time a customer spent waiting versus traditional taxi rides.[12] The superiority of ridesharing is due to simple innovations that taxi drivers have arrogantly ignored. Their success at knowing the streets and routes has blinded them to exciting new ways to understand their trade.

As a consultant who spends significant time in both cabs and ridesharing, I always prefer ridesharing because of the many customer experience reasons I've cited. However, in major cities like Chicago and New York I am frequently forced into taking taxis to and from airports due to their bureaucratic restrictions.

While I was recently in a rush to catch a plane in NYC, my conversation with a cab driver seemed to characterize the position of those in his trade. I was traveling from Wall Street to LaGuardia Airport in New York City, with three viable routes (over three busy bridges) available, any one of which could be best depending on traffic.

Me: LaGuardia Airport please, American Airlines.

Cab driver: Okay, no problem.

Me: What route is quickest now? I need to catch my flight leaving in two hours, so I'm in a rush.

Cab driver: (Appearing miffed that I'm asking questions about the route) I'm going to take the Queens mid-town tunnel.

Me: It looks like there's traffic in midtown, and perhaps

Grand Central Parkway is better now. (I'm looking at my simple map app and can see that traffic on his selected route will increase my travel time by 25 minutes—and he isn't using any app or GPS.)

Cab driver: My way is best now. It's the shortest. If you want something different, you must tell me which way.

Me: Okay, let's try the Grand Central Parkway, please. I'll take responsibility for it being longer if I'm wrong. According to the traffic patterns on my app, it's quicker right now to go Grand Central Parkway. There's something slowing traffic on the route you want to take.

Cab driver: (Doesn't respond.)

Me: Let's go Grand Central Parkway, okay? I'm pressed for time and don't want to get stuck in NYC today.

Cab driver: (Grunts in acknowledgment of my preference.)

After a long period of silence, we arrive at the Grand Central Parkway where the route is clear (and I know I will make my flight).

Me: So how long have you been driving in New York City?

Cab driver: I've had my license for sixteen years now. I am from Kenya and brought my family over.

Me: Do you like driving a cab?

Cab driver: Yes, I like it. I like driving in the daytime on shorter routes. I don't like the airport because I must wait for a trip back. (He then explains his business model, that he shares the car with a partner who drives at night.)

Me: What do you think about Uber?

Cab driver: I don't like Uber. They don't have to pay the fees that I do. They don't have to be checked out like I do.

Me: But aren't they quicker and more convenient for the customer?

Cab driver: They're not professional. They're not good! (Cab driver signals a finality to his statement and ends the conversation with his strong dislike of Uber.)

My NYC cab driver's sentiments are like those of most of the cab drivers I chat with. Usually, I also quietly compare the routes the taxi drivers take compared to the route my apps recommend, and I frequently find that taxi drivers are wrong—just flat wrong in taking the inferior route, due to traffic or distance. I believe their error results from not using GPS or traffic apps that give real-time information about routes, and instead rely on their historical knowledge. Some of the less scrupulous drivers have also acquired the habit of taking the longer pay routes to eke out a little more cab fare. Arrogance and some dishonesty are at play. Regardless, I usually don't try to change their route. However, in the case of the cab driver above, I was in a rush and had to exert more force in my route recommendation. The customer experience of knowing more than the expert, and having to contradict him, denotes a poor one.

Although the cab driver was an expert in NYC traffic and routes, simple innovations—such as a traffic app he chose to ignore—gave me superior knowledge.

Numerous other innovations linked to ride-sharing also add to the taxi industry's dire prognosis. Specific pickup times, car selection, and even early driver identification all exemplify improved features that taxis don't have. Plus, ride-sharing drivers value and thus seek to provide exemplary customer experiences because driver reviews are important to their future success. The crass taxi expertise is being replaced by a friendlier, more informed driver for the ride-sharing experience. These incremental improvements illustrate some of the features propelling ride-sharing services to dominance and killing the traditional taxi model.

CHAPTER 21

Today's Markets: Blue-Chips Are Dead

To most investors, blue chip stocks are a familiar term. First used in the 1920s, blue chips refer to stocks of those companies deemed as the strongest and most viable, both in good markets and bad. The *blue-chip* term comes from the gambling game of poker, where the blue chip is traditionally the highest in value. For a century, blue chip companies have maintained the highest value and have served as a protective hedge against market influences.

However, in the new world of hyper-innovation, no such thing as a guaranteed investment exists anymore. Companies such as Walmart and American Express were once widely viewed as blue chip. But looking at those companies now, one can see the new market pressures they face. Walmart is the king of retail, yet retail is sitting under tremendous pressure from online sales. American Express is the master of travel and credit payments, yet these payment scenarios are facing all manners of credible fintech (financial-technological) disruption.

One merely needs to look at the changing shopping habits of Americans over the last five years to see that Walmart's traditional model is under heavy challenge. In addition to its traditional competitors like Costco, Dollar Tree Stores, and the like, Walmart must deal with an emergent and powerful online challenge that comes from everywhere. Now, customers can price-shop at Walmart and then buy elsewhere if the merchandise is cheaper or delivered for free. In this hyper-innovative world, Walmart has become the shopping site for online retail giants such as Amazon. Consumers can go and view the merchandise at Walmart—even test it out in store—but then buy it online from someone else . . .

cheaper. Walmart remains burdened with a large brick-and-mortar presence while its nimbler online competitors don't have to struggle with operational issues such as rising employee costs or stores operating in different regions.

American Express shares similar challenges, albeit in the financial services sector. With new business models for payment popping up everywhere, American Express must adapt or face extinction. New market entrants such as PayPal or even newer cryptocurrencies are supplanting the traditional business competitors. The advent of cryptocurrency enabled by a technology called blockchain is just one of the many emerging financial payment disruptions occurring. The blue-chip status of American Express, or any traditional company, must face reevaluation in our new markets.

The pace of the world's technological change continues to increase exponentially as well as challenge decades of tradition and expertise previously harbored in blue chip organizations. Now, blue chip companies not only are under the same market scrutiny and risks as the rest of the world, but due to their past successes have greater susceptibility to Victory Disease. While every successful company faces its own idiosyncratic problems, we're now seeing a relentless barrage of change battering blue chips in ways they never strategized could happen.

As a result, the company turnover rate within the Fortune 500 index stands unprecedented. Successful, established companies, now more than ever in history, must prove agile and innovative. The markets in virtually every industry are undergoing major transformational shifts. Over 40 percent of the companies at the top of the Fortune 500 list in 2000 were no longer there in 2010. The following presents a logo snapshot of once-dominant companies that have all lost market share and either are still suffering or have succumbed to the onslaught of Victory Disease:

Logos of once great organizations that have succumbed to Victory Disease

So, what happened to so many great organizations? Numerous case studies or articles point to each decline as related to business, organizational, or market factors. The research and analysis delineate issues such as lack of new products, inability to recognize consumer need changes, and poor management. Those all prove valid factors, but they miss the root causes of the deaths of these companies. Underneath all the business reasons, one or more underlying symptoms of Victory Disease were prominent. Every death includes at least one of the disease symptoms (one of the ABCs) present in their demise.

At one time, organizations could ignore the early symptoms of Victory Disease in favor of running their business; but the unprecedented marketplace changes make Victory Disease even more lethal to those who ignore the warning signs. The hyper-innovation environment makes Victory Disease incredibly lethal, like lung cancer to a smoker. It develops in one part of the organization and quickly metastasizes to infect the organization at large, clasping a tighter and tighter grip on a once healthy company. Much like continued smoke exposure accelerates lung cancer, so the hyper-innovation environment accelerates the spread of Victory Disease. Just as a lung cancer patient must avoid the foundry where the disease developed and find a fresh, clean-air environment, so too must Victory Disease companies avoid the cause of their illness and find a fresh, innovative environment in which to operate. It's simple: ill organizations, like ill people, must abolish the environments that produce their symptoms in order to become healthy. But it's not that easy for ill companies because most of their leaders sit wheezing in denial.

CHAPTER 22

Denial: Why Do Organizations Ignore Victory Disease?

The Blockbuster Corporation offers a prime example of a world-class company that refused to see reality as it lay in the throes of Victory Disease. Blockbuster was a video store monolith that completely dominated the brick-and-mortar video rental market. Unfortunately for them, their business model was disrupted by the advent of technological advancements that made in-person video rentals virtually obsolete. Although Blockbuster saw plenty of warnings as companies like Netflix gained market dominance, their success prevented them from making any major moves toward taking advantage of the new opportunities. At the height of their power in 2004, they boasted over 9,000 stores and 60,000 employees. The size and scope of Blockbuster's business footprint made it difficult for them to entertain new ideas. Overseeing a magnificent bureaucracy of rental efficiency, they sat reluctant to embrace solutions that might impact their large infrastructure.

By the time Blockbuster finally awoke to the many challenges facing them, it was too late. The once dominant video company breathed its last breath just six years after its all-time highest earnings, closing its doors and declaring bankruptcy.

Blockbuster's demise is well known by its dominant presence and subsequent lost stores in just about every major American city. What isn't so well known is that it could have completely avoided catching the disease in the first place if it had only self-administered an antidote. Innovation opportunities abounded, such as new technologies, partnerships, and other avenues that would have saved them. Like so many great companies, the opportunity to capitalize on new innovations and networks sat within reach, but they simply didn't think they needed to adapt or make the effort.

Blockbuster's arrogance and complacency were on display in their dealings with the company Netflix. We all know that Netflix was one of their primary disruptors. But what most people don't know is that before the Netflix business model killed the mighty Blockbuster, Netflix sought a partnership with them. In 2000, the Netflix founder, Reed Hastings, visited Blockbuster headquarters to propose a partnership to the Blockbuster leadership team. Hastings offered to share his social networks and business model by carrying the Blockbuster brand online in exchange for Netflix promotion in Blockbuster's stores. There was ample opportunity for all to benefit, and the partnership would have been good for both the emerging Netflix and the megacompany Blockbuster. But the vision of Blockbuster's leadership was overshadowed by the arrogance of retail excellence. After all, they were masters of the retail video rental space with a long history of success. Just as the Japanese failed to recognize the disruptive importance of airpower, the Blockbuster leadership did not recognize the importance of social and online videos. And while many variables were at play, as in all business models, Blockbuster chose to bypass any collaboration with the new rental model in its early stages, the type of decision that would ultimately kill them.

Many of us witnessed what happened as Blockbuster atrophied away into nothingness, with Victory Disease's hold on the mighty company starving it out of existence. As more and more customers opted for an online or sharing model, Blockbuster stores became more and more malnourished. At a certain point in their demise, the video rental chain focused on trying to sell ancillary candy and movie products out of their storefronts. While ignoring the social epidemic besieging the video rental business,

Blockbuster sold candy. People wanted a say in how they rented and where they rented, including flexibility in how long they rented for, while Blockbuster offered them a lollipop. They languished in denial of real customer desires, unable to escape their view that they were the experts with an incredibly efficient video rental process that would somehow carry them forward. Arrogance and hubris were clearly at play. Fast forward to today: Netflix is now a mighty $125 billion company commanding the video-on-demand market, and the once dominant Blockbuster enjoys just one insignificant store still open in Oregon.

The last Blockbuster store in Bend, Oregon; the number of Blockbuster employees nationwide was 84,300 in 2004; 25,000 in 2010; and three in 2019[13]

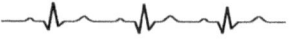

Practical Reflection: The Death Spiral

The *death spiral* refers to continually descending sales accompanied by increasing costs that eventually lead to an organization's demise. In business lingo, it's frequently called the *downward demand spiral*. It happens when a business loses sales but doesn't proportionately decrease their costs. The business then has to increase the cost of their goods or services to cover the "increased" costs, which then causes them to sell less because of higher set prices. If more sales don't occur or costs aren't lowered, the business continues to descend until they finally become insolvent. Conventional business school wisdom teaches young leaders to counter the death spiral by tightly managing costs and reducing the costs of the organization proportionate to the lost revenue. Unfortunately, this, too, results in ultimate insolvency (but keeps the organization alive a bit longer).

What business schools miss completely is the need to innovate *outside* the product lifecycle. In the rational business school world, educators tend not to advance their ideas beyond the dollars and cents of an issue. They teach the implications of pricing decisions and how to reduce costs—with managerial accounting classes spending weeks discussing the death spiral— without ever demonstrating how to leverage real solutions other than incremental ways to run the business. Most times the death spiral is heavily influenced by psychological factors such as those present in the Victory Disease ABCs, but these factors aren't discussed. The solution to the death spiral isn't more stringent management controls that just prolong the inevitable. The real solution lies in prudent risk-taking and innovation.

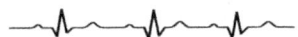

CHAPTER 23
Innovation: The Buzzword vs Reality

Leaders love the sound and use of the term *innovation* and have made it a huge buzzword. Most buzzword users simply love the front end of innovation. Meaning, they don't have much backbone for the real work required to launch innovation, but just like to think and talk about it. The risks and failures do not attract but repel them. You can describe many leaders as political animals who've gained their positions through political posturing and maneuvering. The front end of innovation supports their posturing and greatly enhances their image. They don't really understand innovation's entire process, just merely that some people have leveraged it successfully and thus that supporting it publicly can be a nice thing. They are the leaders who keep a handful of popular innovation books on their bookcase behind their desk but don't really practice the methodologies. This scenario translates into organizational leaders who support the front-end activities with talk but lack the depth to truly care about ideas once the innovations are ready to prototype and build. Because new advances and startups fail without real support, the ideas and programs that support those advances frequently fail in successful organizations that are not truly committed to innovation.

As an innovation strategist, one of the first things I try to do is understand an organization's goals. I like to chat with senior leaders about their strategic objectives. During that talk, I ask them if they support innovation. Without question, every single leader says they do, most definitely. Doing so is sexy and cool, as well as essential to the lifeblood of organizational growth, which cause them all to *say* that they support innovation. But then I like to dig deeper to see who are the real supporters and change agents, and who are the pretenders. After warming them up by asking them their definition of innovation and what innovative opportunities they see, I ask them, *"If someone were to provide a potential breakthrough idea to solve your business challenges, would you be willing to support it with your time, your organization's budget, and people resources?"*

It's at this question that I lose most of them with excuses such as, "Well, my project budget is all full . . ." or "Gee, I recently lost one-third of my organization to off-shore work . . ." or a whole host of other excuses. They are the leaders that find the front end of innovation attractive, a way to enhance their reputation as a cutting-edge trendsetter, but they aren't willing to really do any of the work required to make change happen.

But occasionally I do find a leader willing to support ideas with their time and resources. When that occurs, I know I have a supportive leader before me who may be capable of making some good things happen. I then ask the final question to determine if they are truly leaders: *"Would you be willing to not just support the effort with time and resources, but personally champion the effort, including publicly discussing your lessons learned if it fails?"* At this point in my interview dialogue, I've lost at least 90 percent of the leaders. However, I know I've found true innovation champions in those that agree to support change and different solutions all the way through, even to the point of potential failure. Those are the leaders that I focus on and build innovation efforts around. The front-end folks who merely want to appear innovative because it's attractive are the leaders I avoid. They are the ones who will contribute to the demise of a company organization by constantly finding fault with innovation execution. They will be all about the ideas but nothing about building or really learning from those ideas. They aren't willing to take chances apart from the official, risk-averse plan.

Therefore, all innovation programs need a strategic effort behind them in addition to the organizational plan. Innovation results should not be part of any annual plan for revenue or growth. It puts too much stress on the innovation organization and allows the innovation naysayers within the organization (and there are lots of them) to have a business reason to cut innovation.

I recently worked with a large tax preparation company notably infected with Victory Disease that couldn't come to terms with the fact it had the illness. Because of their denial, I fully expect they will die within the next 10 years, even though they are currently one of the tax preparation leaders in the U.S., with a decent market share. In fact, they have enjoyed a long history of victories and success.

Yet, during my initial interviews, many of their leaders could see their long streak of victories were coming to an end, and so could I. Their business model was one in which they occupied numerous local storefronts during tax season and had tens of thousands of tax preparers on their books—and they were successful. However, the rise of online tax preparation software, like Intuit's TurboTax, had started to reduce their customer base. I was friends with some of the Intuit leaders and knew they are not only relentlessly improving their online products but planning to make their direct offerings simpler and cheaper as well . . . until they engulf most of the market. TurboTax, at the time, was not suffering from Victory Disease and was on a campaign to incrementally create a "wow" tax experience. Meanwhile, other even more disruptive personal finance software options were emerging that further streamlined and simplified the tax preparation process for the middle class.

Since my client tax preparer company had no innovation leader per se, the human resources leader served as my point of contact. As she put it, they wanted to "speed up their transformation process." My task was to interview their key senior leaders, including their CEO, and then we would develop their new innovation strategy. As I worked my way through the interviews, a common theme emerged recognizing the diminishing market. I was happy that their leadership was acknowledging they had a problem—complacency and arrogance didn't appear an issue for them. That is, until I interviewed the CEO, the last holdout.

Most of the other leaders had pointed to the CEO as the man who needed to agree with a transformational effort for the organization. But no one warned me that he might not be on board. After conducting the other leader interviews, my assumption was that the company leadership recognized that their platform was burning. This acknowledgment was essential to true transformation. But when I spoke with the CEO, I was struck by his unwillingness to change. His leadership team had all recognized their dwindling market, and the CEO reluctantly acknowledged it also. But he was affected by something different.

He told me he was fully dedicated to the 40,000-plus full- and part-time employees of their organization and wouldn't do anything to harm them. He also told me he was willing to spend only up to 5 percent of his time on new endeavors because he had his hands full running the organization. This response proved problematic since he was identified as THE man at the heart of any change. So, during the interviews I probed deeper into his thinking. He acknowledged he could see their market share dwindling, their profit margins decreasing, and even their market change so they were now targeting mostly the lower socioeconomic classes. Yet, he wasn't willing to make more time for innovation nor even explore possibilities that might change their human resources model. He was essentially *innovation blocking*.

I recognized in the CEO a special type of arrogance that can affect large, successful organizations. This illustrated the personal arrogance of leaders who receive large salaries and bonuses that aren't tied to change and transformation. The hassle and risk of the change simply aren't worthwhile to the leader. Even though the organization was clearly diseased and slowly dying, that inevitable scenario wasn't really going to affect him personally. He was still going to make his humongous salary, pocket a bonus, and likely be gone prior to the company's demise. He enjoyed the responsibility of running a large enterprise and reaping the love of his employees, so he saw no value in introducing change. In other words, life was good for him personally, so he could ignore the company's long-term illness. He topped off his arrogance by telling me he wouldn't consider any changes that might radically affect the business model. Because of his desire to maintain the status quo, my innovation engagement abruptly came to an end.

The problem of the tax preparation service lay in the self-centered arrogance often found with senior leaders of successful organizations. These leaders don't have to care for the long-term welfare of their organization because they are well-liked and personally secure. The senior leadership ranks of successful companies, especially publicly traded ones, comprise a multi-millionaire's club of very wealthy and comfortable people. Life is good for them, so long-term organizational health does not top their priority list if it puts their personal comfort at risk. What is worse, their personal goals frequently incentivize them to remain short-term minded, which diminishes their desire for transformational change. While this situation was far from the case with the original Victory Disease folks (Japanese military leaders cared about the organization more than themselves), it definitely becomes an occurrence with leaders of successful money-oriented organizations.

Jeff Bezos of Amazon is an example of a leader who gets it, and because of that insight, his organization thrives. He holds a long-standing philosophy of *Day 1* thinking and actions as the key to staying relevant. By Day 1 he means constantly thinking and acting in new ways with regards to customer needs and experiences. He then refers to *Day 2* as "stasis . . . followed by irrelevance." Bezos' Day 2 is where Victory Disease symptoms take hold. You can easily see the positive results of having a CEO that understands the nature of the dreaded disease. He even wrote a letter to the Amazon board that describes his *Day 1* and *Day 2* thinking, which is attached as an Appendix.

CHAPTER 24

Victory Disease Poster Child: Kodak

The Eastman Kodak company offers a prime example of a very successful company that ignored changes in the marketplace and didn't lead, or even fast-follow, the digital photo trend until too late. Kodak was master of the 20th century camera and film processing market. They were incredible. They dominated the market, with their brand name even widely associated with key life events. We called them "Kodak moments" when our cameras captured important celebrations and times we wanted to impress in our memories, and we asked others to "Kodak it" when requesting just such a photo. Kodak became part of the American language, a verb, adjective, and noun that took that market leadership to new heights. Their established processes in developing film became models of modern efficiency. They could reliably develop pictures to the highest levels of quality within minutes—a remarkable feat. Kodak transformed the film processing landscape and became the undisputed champion of film.

Unfortunately for them, the digital camera innovation came along in the 1970s, which (as we know) revolutionized image capturing and practically eliminated film processing technology. But Kodak's demise wasn't about technology; that was just the contributing factor. Kodak's demise was due to Victory Disease— they were reveling so much in their success and established strategies that they couldn't capitalize on the emerging business models and new technology.

In fact, one of the first digital cameras was invented and patented in 1975 by a man named Steve Sasson, an engineer with Kodak. But then—through a rather long series of mistakes and oversights—Kodak sat on the digital image idea and let others take the lead. Sasson later related that a senior Kodak leader responded to his invention with "that's cute, but don't tell anyone about it."[14] This attitude resulted, in large part, from their superior processes that were netting the company incredible revenues. Kodak's film processing bureaucracy was the best in the business. Their "victory" in film processing prevented them from seeing or capitalizing on the massive opportunity in digital.

Steve Jobs would have been good for Kodak at that time. He was well known for his ability to teach the philosophy of disrupting one's own company before someone else does. He knew that once ideas become concrete enough to form prototypes and tests, you can no longer ignore or hide them. Coincidentally, Steve Jobs was indirectly involved with Kodak's demise as the emergence of digital photography, combined with the emergence of the iPhone, ultimately created a one-two punch that put Kodak on the ground.

As with almost every case of Victory Disease, it needn't be so. Kodak didn't need to die, or even shrink . . . they needed to grow. Healthy options were readily available for Kodak if only they wanted to transform. We merely need to look to their biggest competitor, Fuji, to see how a successful company used their previous victories to propel them to new heights in the digital age. Fuji, a Japanese company headquartered in Tokyo, was the second largest film developer in the late 20th century, next to Kodak. But Fuji did not rest on their laurels or try to ignore the emerging digital epidemic. Instead, they self-administered an antidote. Fuji assessed the competitive landscape, saw it changing, and made aggressive moves to adapt their management and business model structures to support those changes. They developed new digital products, created entrepreneurial partnerships, and transformed from film to digital. Now, Fuji lists innovation as one if its core values and derives great benefit from its self-administered antidote. Their involvement in digital imagery, optics, imaging, and graphic arts are all results of a transformational mindset that avoided the stagnation of Kodak. While Fuji's organizational changes weren't easy or perfect, they survived nicely and are now thriving, with approximately 80,000 employees and $22 billion annual net income.[15]

Unfortunately, by the time Eastman Kodak woke up in the early 21st century, their Victory Disease had become terminal. The market was full of motivated competitors who held a large market share. Fast followers like Fuji were hard to overcome. Although Kodak was an early and reluctant pioneer in the digital space, and is frequently credited with inventing the digital camera, Victory Disease forced them to file for bankruptcy in 2012.

When a Fire Is Raging
Flee, Fight, or Fry

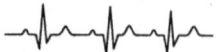

If you want something new, you have to stop
doing something old."
—Peter F. Drucker

CHAPTER 25
The Burning Platform

To begin the healing process through innovation, leaders must first recognize that their organizations are in trouble. I sometimes refer to this as the *burning platform* for innovation. Burning platform is a business metaphor for a dire circumstance that requires immediate strategic action. When an oil platform is burning in the middle of the ocean, a sense of urgency for immediate change seems to engulf everyone involved. The platform occupants have only a handful of options. They can abandon the platform, try to put out the fire, or stay in place and call for help. If the required action isn't implemented, death will likely follow. And thus, a burning platform paints the perfect metaphor for most organizations in the throes of Victory Disease. Sometimes the first critical step lies in organizations understanding that some or all of the ABCs of Victory Disease are ablaze around them—that they are, indeed, standing on a burning platform.

Practical Reflection:

The Burning Platform Origins of "Either Jump or Fry"

On a July evening in 1988, at about 9:30 p.m., a disastrous explosion and fire erupted on the Piper Alpha oil-drilling platform in the North Sea, off the coast of Scotland. Two rescuers and 166 crew members lost their lives in what was (and still is) the worst catastrophe in the fifty-year history of North Sea oil exportation. One of the sixty-three crew members who survived was Andy Mochan, a superintendent on the rig.

From the hospital, Mochan told of being awakened by the explosion and alarms. Badly injured, he escaped from his quarters to the platform edge. Beneath him, oil had surfaced and ignited. Twisted steel and other debris littered the surface of the water. He considered the risk of jumping. Dangerous debris was all over the surface. Because of the water's cold temperature, he knew he could live a maximum of only twenty minutes if he missed the debris. Despite all that, Andy jumped fifteen stories from the platform to the water. And . . . he survived . . . because . . . he jumped.

When asked why he took that potentially fatal leap, he did not hesitate to say, "It was either jump or fry." He chose possible death over certain death. Andy jumped because he realized he had no choice—the price of staying on the platform was too high. This was how we arrived at the term "burning platform."

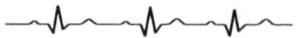

It's very difficult to institute change without recognizing the need for change. Like the Japanese bushido, the positive aspects of tradition can stifle altering views. In many organizations, the burning platform isn't recognized to be on fire and the organization resists change.

CHAPTER 26

Save Your Organization by Starting a Fire

One of the most tragic and innovative examples in firefighting involves the story of the Mann Gulch fire and the firefighting foreman's actions on that fateful day. In August 1949, a massive, out-of-control wildfire swept through Mann Gulch, Montana. Fifteen professional fire jumpers were deployed to try to bring the fire under control. All young men, they were led by their foreman, a man named Wagner "Wag" Dodge, the oldest of the group at age 33.

The men were airdropped onto the top of the gulch, where they made plans for extinguishing the fire, starting with their normal procedures for firefighting. But soon after, amidst the fight, they saw the wind and atmosphere change so that the fire began crossing behind them, climbing up the hill from where they came. Leading the men at the front of their line, Wag saw the fire coming up and over them, and so started leading his men back up the gulch. By its nature, fire moves swiftly up hill, and the fire quickly encompassed the fatigued firefighters.

Once Wag and his men realized the fire was surrounding them, it became a footrace. Future reports estimated that the fire on the gulch was burning at about 1,700 degrees Fahrenheit and moving at 660 feet per minute—way too fast to simply outrun. Although Wag was not an engineer, he was an experienced firefighter and widely awakened to the fact that they had seconds to do something different. And so Wag did something unique, something no one in the firefighting business had ever done or even talked about doing—he started a fire to try to save himself from a fire.

Wag took out a match and lit a fire in front of him. The scorching heat and high winds caused his fire to immediately burn off a hundred feet of land before him. And then he ran into the middle of the still smoldering area he had just burned. Wag yelled for his men to join him in the middle of his fire patch, but no one did. Follow-on reports stated some men didn't hear him, others thought he'd gone crazy, and one man was reported to have yelled, "To hell with that!" All of Wag's men continued running up the gulch to try to outrace the fire.

Wag, on the other hand, went to the smoldering area of the middle of his fire and lay face-down in the burnt, black grass he had just scorched. Wag would later say he thought his chance of survival at "more than even." Almost immediately, the main fire encompassed his area. All the men lost their vision in the smoke, which caused them to run wildly, hoping to find a crevasse or hole in the fire. Five men initially made it out alive, two by running and two who stumbled upon a rock clearing. But because of bodily damages from the vicious fire, only two of them survived, with the others eventually succumbing to burns and smoke inhalation.

Only Wag came out unscathed. The massive fire quickly reached close to Wag, who lay face-down in the middle of his fire patch, yet the fire couldn't find any fuel to continue moving that way, so it eventually moved around Wag's position and on up the hill. After about 15 minutes of protecting himself face-down, Wag stood up, assessed that the fire had passed him, and walked away uninjured out of the ashes of his own fire.

What Wag did was to burn a path in the fire by using fire. In a metaphorical sense, Wag used the same source that was threatening to kill his team to defeat that threat. He fought fire with fire. This concept was unheard of in American firefighting at the time. Wag had seen the trouble they were in, accurately assessed the options, and took a calculated risk on a rapid innovation. It's not the kind of risk anyone would want to take, to risk one's life, but the situation demanded radical actions. Wag wasn't afraid to use the very thing that was pursuing him as a solution to his dilemma because he recognized that the rules of the game had changed so much. Thus, he simply had to try something different on the gulch that day. And it worked. Much like present day organizations fighting fires the same old way, Wag's team couldn't make sense of Wag wanting to disrupt the status quo of firefighting by starting a fire. Wag's team was trying to use incrementalism to stop the fire—to spray the fire with water over and over again in order to direct and eventually stop its path; and to run from it when too close. Certainly, this incrementalism frequently works with fires.

However, Wag had the presence of mind to know that a more innovative solution was required, and he wasn't afraid to try it. More and more in today's organizations, survival requires creative thinking and risk-taking, and most importantly, a willingness to disrupt your own business model. Although he was a fire-jumping foreman from sixty years ago, Wag Dodge shows us the path organizations may have to forge to survive today.

It's All About Change

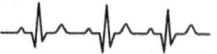

"The secret of change is to focus all of your energy,
not on fighting the old, but building on the new."
                                                    —Socrates

CHAPTER 27
Incremental Change

As illustrated in the Wag Dodge story, incremental change doesn't usually work with Victory Disease. Incrementalism is characterized by making small changes to existing products or services. Sometimes it's called *core* or *adjacent* innovation because small changes are made to the core of the business, but the central aspects of a company's model remain unaffected. Yet usually by the time an organization sees the symptoms of Victory Disease, a drastic change is necessary. Many companies continue with an incremental approach, as they always have, trying a slight change or building an adjacent product line—nothing too drastic because they're completely wed to their current model, but a change that reflects their previous success applied in a similar way.

For an insurance company, incrementalism could mean introducing a new product that is like others they have; if they sell life insurance, perhaps they explore a new life insurance product. Or for a clothes retailer, incrementalism could mean a new line of clothing. In banking, one can see brick-and-mortar banks making incremental changes by redesigning their branches to reflect a more user-friendly approach, perhaps more Apple store like. The upkeep of brick-and-mortar locations is one of the things killing them, but they can't let go of this mindset so they make incremental changes rather than explore significant transformation.

But unlike days gone by, the current business environment is simply changing too rapidly, no matter what field or market, and incrementalism is simply too weak, too lackluster, not enough.

Take Frederick's of Hollywood, the once dominant lingerie

powerhouse that recently closed all its stores. The 70-year-old company was founded in the 1950s' pin-up era, when a winning formula included images of beautiful women, direct mail catalogues, and well-placed storefronts. But as the environment changed, the Internet became king and catalogues became obsolete; yet Fredericks chose to pursue incremental change as a recovery strategy. As they didn't dare pursue the hard changes necessary, their main Victory Disease symptom was complacency. The CEO, Frederick Mellinger, set the tone for the complacent environment with his famous quote, "Sex never goes out of fashion." Significant changes would mean they needed to change the central way they operated through catalogues and stores.

Instead, they stuck with their catalogue model and tried to give it a younger, more contemporary feel. For their flagship innovative product, they launched an adjacent brand called Harriett, designed to target the "accessible luxury" market. Yet, it was the same thing in a different package. Although Frederick's could see the changes in the industry occurring, they chose to stick with their previous success and make only incremental changes, even in the face of their own death. Complacency caused one of the iconic and most recognizable brands in the world to file for bankruptcy in 2000. They re-emerged in 2003, only to succumb to Victory Disease in 2015, by closing all 111 of their stores. They succumbed to Victory Disease by just trying to survive incrementally, making no significant changes to their business model.

CHAPTER 28

Disruptive Innovation: Current Innovation Theory Doesn't Go Far Enough

Clayton Christensen is credited with bringing the term *disruptive innovation* into our mainstream business lexicon. The concept of disruptive innovation is a marvelous acknowledgement that radical change in markets comes from business model changes among competing organizations. The disruption, according to his theory, begins in brand-new markets or in markets where the number of customers and economic benefits are tepid, not rising to significant levels. Viewing these new markets or lower-end markets with disinterest, businesses that are already successful don't catch on to the burgeoning opportunities residing there. Yet because a new market demands that organizations develop a new business model, the emergent companies thrive in these new markets as they build market share. Meanwhile, the old market leaders are too slow to recognize the economic benefits of the new market. Ultimately, the new companies with their new business models overtake the incumbent leaders and become the new market leaders. Hence, disruptive innovation is a process involving new business models.

Christensen's theory is extremely compelling and, in my opinion, true. I have witnessed it positively influencing the understanding of business-change across the world. However, it stops short of being truly descriptive because it misses the root causes of the disruption. By sterilely dissecting the process of disruption, Christensen's theory misses the underlying reasons why successful companies don't change. Christensen, a life-long academician, sees the problem in a very academic way. The underlying human and organizational causes are not explored, even though they are the root triggers of the problem. If Christensen had taken it one step further to identify the root sources, he would have stumbled upon the human causes of arrogance and complacency, as well as the structural cause of bureaucracy.

If we use Kodak as an example, Christensen's theory would have us believe that Kodak's death was primarily due to the emergence of the digital market. That Kodak didn't see it coming because the market was under-served and unappetizing. And that Kodak failed to recognize the importance of digital imagery until too late. But we now know differently. We know that Kodak was able to identify the new digital trend and even invented the first digital camera. In fact, Vincent Barabba, former head of market intelligence at Kodak, detailed in his book *Decision Loom* that all Kodak leaders knew about the impact of digital photography in the early 1980s.[16] So, if the leaders knew the impending impact of digital imagery and did nothing, there had to be a deeper reason they didn't act. And, as we've examined, there absolutely was.

The Kodak leaders, as well as other successful organization leaders, are not nearly as rational as Christensen's theory would have us believe. They are human, subject to the same temptations of life that all humans are. Organizations and their leaders are not as cogent nor single-minded as Christensen's disruptive theory would have us believe. In this respect, Christensen's disruptive theory disproves itself. If organizations are rational and merely don't recognize the new markets, then when they finally do recognize them, we should see them acting quickly. Since Christensen's theory has been widely accepted and used, then it would follow that successful organizations would since have adapted to account for the emerging markets. That they have adjusted to take advantage of the emerging or new underserved customers in order to stay dominant. But they haven't. As discussed in this book, market leaders have been crashing at an even faster pace, with more and more new organizations assuming market leadership. The root cause of this change isn't an inability to recognize changes, but can be traced to the ABCs of Victory Disease. The real root causes of successful organizations dying stem from arrogance, bureaucracy and complacency.

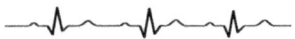

Practical Reflection: Outside the Box

Thinking "outside the box" is an often-used phrase in the innovation world. We all have heard it, and it's a very appropriate term to use for finding solutions that don't conform to traditional methods or thinking. But few know that it came from a mentally challenging puzzle that requires the solver to actually find a solution lying literally outside the box. Below is the puzzle; you'll find the solution in the Appendix. **Hint:** it's solved by moving the four connecting lines so they are outside the box of options.

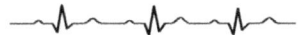

Connect the dots below using only four lines and going through each dot exactly once.

CHAPTER 29

Exponential Growth Is the New Norm

In this crazy, hyper-innovation environment, an amazing phenomenon is happening, and I am happy to be an innovation practitioner as it occurs. I can only describe that phenomenon as an innovation explosion unlike any in world history. It's directly related to the extraordinary power of exponential growth, combined with the evolution of our information collaboration methods. Innovation is happening at a faster-than-ever, break-neck speed—and it doesn't just *feel* like it's happening faster; it absolutely *is* happening faster. Yet for those companies that don't embrace change, the phenomenon is forever disrupting their existing business models and accelerating the growth of Victory Disease.

Exponential growth and the technology revolution have been written about extensively, with Moore's Law most frequently mentioned. Moore's Law is the information technology prediction of Gordon Moore, whereby he predicted the doubling of components for circuitry every two years. This technology circuitry doubling proved to be true and, consequently, demonstrated many other applications related to technological innovation. It was, and remains, a great example of the rapidity of technological growth. I would even argue that Moore's initial 2X law has been surpassed, with a growth rate even faster in certain cases. This growth offers a great opportunity for large companies that are agile and accepting of change, and a real problem for companies sitting in the throes of Victory Disease.

Moore's Law was made more understandable when Ray Kurzweil wrote about the "Law of Accelerating Returns" and used the *Chessboard and Rice* parable. He refers to the story about an ancient King who wants to honor the inventor of chess. The King loves the game and desires to reward the inventor. The King offers the chess inventor anything he wants. The crafty inventor merely asks for rice—a single grain to start with. He asks for a single grain of rice to be placed on the first square of the chessboard, and then doubled for each successive square until all the squares have rice. The first square has one grain, the second square two grains, the third square four grains, and so on, until all sixty-four squares have their share of rice doubled from the previous square. The King thinks this a very small reward for the invention of such a great game.

Nonetheless, he approves of the request and orders the rice be doubled on each square of the chessboard for the inventor. Well, the rice amounts don't add up to much for the first half of the chessboard as they are doubled for each square, but moving into the second half, the amounts start getting large. Really, really large. The rice amount becomes larger than the room, and soon outpaces all the rice production in the entire Kingdom. The point of the story lies in the incredible multiplicity effect of routinely doubling amounts. That effect is occurring now with our various technologies and having the same effects. In the story, everyone realizes the allocation of rice exceeds the Kingdom's capacity, and since the King's decrees are irreversible, the inventor becomes King. Much like innovation, the *Chess and Rice* story has a different outcome, depending on the country where it's told. Sometimes it ends with the inventor owning the Kingdom, and sometimes it ends with the inventor losing his head (I prefer the former version).

Mathematically, the exponential growth of the rice ends up

being 2^{63} which is a whole lot of rice, more rice than available in the whole Kingdom. But a mathematical formula is hard to imagine. It's easier to imagine how much that really is if we considered it extending into outer space. Picture this: if the rice were stacked into a large tower that was 125 feet square, it would rise all the way to the moon. The exponential growth of all forms of technology is one of the major impacts to our external business environment.

Unfortunately, most successful organizations don't anticipate exponential growth. They are all about incremental growth. They have processes and systems and methodologies to continue their business. They are very good at the old thing that brought them into business and usually very bad at building new things that could exponentially grow their business. Existing organizations prove victorious because they manage their scarce resources well, so they feel like it's a scarce resource environment. They plod along on a linear path of growth, trying to eke out a new product or service while devoting most of their attention to running the existing business. In their world of assuming continued success, leaders are hired and promoted based on how well they know and can manage the business within the constraints of budget and personnel. So, when they are tasked with growth, they incrementally work with what they know and plan for the scarcity of resources to eke out another widget.

To compare existing, successful growth with the prospect of exponential growth, let's examine a lodging and hotel industry example. InterContinental Hotels Group is a global hotel chain that has been very successful (and is where I frequently choose to stay). But when InterContinental wants to grow, they employ a process and formula that plans for a new place and location. They have to conduct surveys, seek financing, conduct cost-benefit analysis on whether to build new or buy an existing structure, and align with whole host of other scarcity requirements. The InterContinental Hotels can obviously grow and continue their success, but growth is laborious and slow, not exponential. They have decided to limit themselves to the finite world of what is possible within their existing resources.

By contrast, look at a new market entrant like Airbnb, the short-term rental organization that operates exponentially and can expand into new markets without concern for most of InterContinental's limitations, or at least the ones InterContinental thinks are mandatory. Because Airbnb doesn't place most of the organizational restrictions on itself that traditional hoteliers like InterContinental do, it is able to grow exponentially with much less effort. The advancement and growth into new areas doesn't require the traditional management of resources. Airbnb leverages the social and online marketplace to connect people who own places with people who want to use them. It's simple, yet effective. Hosts provide their places for use, and travelers use them. Airbnb, as the managing organization, doesn't require locations, research, massive construction, or most of the other scarcity limitations that InterContinental has placed on themselves. At one time, those limitations would have prevented Airbnb from operating, but in the new business environment enabled by the information age and accelerated technologies, it's infinitely simpler for Airbnb to grow. Once limited to serving thrifty tourists looking for a bargain, the sharing economy has enabled the growth of Airbnb models. Much like *the Rice and Chessboard* story, as entrepreneurial organizations start stacking rice in these new endeavors, they find that they can increase their growth exponentially. If Airbnb wants to grow by 10,000 rooms in a specific location, they merely need to find 10,000 hosts to offer up their places. Because of new technologies and the abundance of options they allow, the rules of the game have changed. And yet established hoteliers either can't, or don't, change their business models to play with the new rules. It's not a fair game anymore when some of the participants are victim to scarcity operations, and some aren't.

CHAPTER 30
Unlimited Catalysts for Change

The amounts and types of innovations currently being launched are unprecedented in the history of the world. More amazing innovations will be created during this generation than in all of history. Not only is technology increasing exponentially, but knowledge is increasing at unprecedented rates. The global network and the ability to instantly share information are shifting the landscape of virtually every public and private market in the world—change is unlimited. Yet with massive changes come massive threats—and those from non-traditional competitors are now an ever-present stressor for successful businesses, small and large. New market entrants are scaling at record-breaking rates. The hyper-innovation environment is flipping former business models and theories on their heads.

Innovation historically has come in progressively quicker waves; now, a sea of constant transformation is upon us. The exponential pace of change from innovations provides us a daily realization of the *Chessboard and Rice* parable. The sharing economy is being used to sidestep traditional processes and exponentially grow value through sharing.

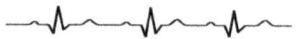

Practical Case: Friendsurance
The startup Friendsurance gives an example of an emerging sharing-economy innovation that threatens current business models. It intrigues me because it's in my market of financial services, where conservatism and regulation regularly try to stomp out new ideas. Yet Friendsurance is a hole-in-one—a disruptive idea that has launched successfully and now has the potential to change the stodgy insurance industry.

Friendsurance, as their name states, underwrites insurance for friends. They have combined the growing online social aspects of today's environment with the need for insurance. They have fundamentally gotten to the real core of what insurance was invented for and has always been: a way for us to protect each other from unexpected events that we cannot afford by ourselves. It's a beautiful concept because it's the reason insurance started and the reason that insurance companies have names like Farmers and State Farm, which were started by and for farmers. But unlike the insurance giants that now dominate the market, technology and the sharing economy have allowed peer-to-peer startups to return to the roots of insurance, where we know the people whom we are underwriting. Whereas the giant companies now have super complicated pools and algorithms that they use to group their insurance clients, Friendsurance merely allows people to group with people they know, usually close friends and family.

The result is a positive insurance experience where policyholders look out for each other and care for each other. Along with the positive experience comes lower premiums (because fraud is reduced) as well as incentives for not filing claims. People don't cheat their friends and family, and this social insurance model builds nicely on that principle. Friendsurance launched in Germany and has expanded to Australia. Though not yet available in the U.S., I suspect that it or a similar model will be here soon. Disruption is international.

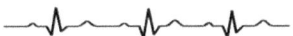

Besides a sharing economy, other major drivers of unprecedented change include the growing list of disruptive innovations such as artificial intelligence, virtual/augmented reality, cybersecurity, blockchain, a connected world, and the social media explosion. And this list is growing rapidly. All these amazing, emerging innovations are making big impacts and big changes, which affect the environment in which organizations must exist.

Over the past few years, startups, incubators and accelerators, capitalizing on these changes, are growing rapidly. New international companies and innovations are exploding onto the market with no end in sight. Small, community-based programs supporting the growth of local businesses have played a huge role in the spread of startup fever across the world. Not surprisingly, smart organizations are aware of the emerging trends and are approaching them with openness and ingenuity. Organizations under the throes of Victory Disease are not.

CHAPTER 31
Avoiding the Shiny Object Syndrome

Innovation proves a powerful tool in the fight against Victory Disease, but some common traps often catch unsuspecting organizations as they try to overcome the illness. One such trap is the *shiny object syndrome*. The shiny object syndrome is the problem of distraction, chasing too many attractive things at once with no focus. In this world of hyper-innovations, the syndrome illustrates one of the most common traps for an organization trying to overcome its problems. I compare it to a child who is distracted chasing shiny objects. Also referred to as chasing squirrels, this common trap gets the organization to find so many attractive solutions that it pursues them all. Ultimately, the finite resources of the organization are exhausted, with nothing coming to fruition; its resources are all expended in discovering and experimenting with the new ideas—yet implementing none of them.

In my innovation consulting practice, shiny object syndrome is the number one problem I encounter with new innovation programs. The well-meaning leadership devotes employees and resources to propel their organization out of their malaise, but the shiny objects are too many and too powerful for them to ignore. They end up endlessly exploring each of them and wasting their resources on the front end of product development, with nothing to show on the back end.

This brings up a very real problem that exists with innovation: it's attractive in some stages and very unappealing in others. That push and pull—between the attractiveness and ugliness of innovation—is a powerful factor in an organization's inability to overcome Victory Disease. Here is why: innovation and new ideas seem very attractive at the start of the ideation process and very ugly at the end. The start of innovation involves ideas, free-flowing creativity, and fun. It's where breakthroughs come and billion-dollar ideas are created. The world-changing ideas start in the front end, and we all love to look back and point to the original idea while ignoring all the hard work it took to make it successful. In contrast to the ideation stage, the back end of innovation involves hard work, failures, and lessons. It's like making sausage; it's an ugly process. It's where project teams should conduct due diligence, lawyers should wrestle with laws and regulations, operators should modify approaches, and those creative ideas should be made reality. The front end of innovation is sexy and appealing, while the back end of innovation is hard work, failure, and change. When the leaders of organizations look at innovation, they, like all of us, make choices based on attractiveness. They gravitate toward the front end, the creative and fun side of innovation, and avoid the ugly back end.

A couple of long-running, popular innovation conferences in the United States provide good examples of the popularity differences between creating ideas and then actually seeing them through. Two separate, long-running conferences are titled "Front End of Innovation" and "Back End of Innovation." Organized by the same group using the same marketing techniques, the Front-End Conference is supposed to be about the front-end activities, and the Back-End Conference about the back-end activities. I have spoken at them both numerous times and even been on their advisory board. What I have observed is that everyone loves the front end of innovation, making the Front-End Conference very large in attendees, while the Back-End Conference is way less popular and struggles to draw half as many attendees. Even with the very clear topics for each conference, people who attend and speak at the Back-End Conference have a tough time staying focused on the back end, preferring to stray into the more exciting area of idea development.

In a broad sense, every organization has fantastic ideas. Many wonderful ideas flicker out there in the universe of possibilities, and they are exciting to consider. The real challenge comes from doing something with those ideas. Front-end innovation brings excitement and creativity. Everyone loves to talk about the origin of great ideas. How Steve Jobs revolutionized the personal computer, or Thomas Edison invented the modern light. Ideas are fun and sexy.

Back-end innovation is not so sexy. It requires hard work that involves knowledgeable people, functioning processes, working systems, and funding; yet even with all of this considered, there is no guarantee of success. Analysts estimate that nine out of ten new business ideas fail. The concept that good ideas launch themselves is a myth. Sausage is a wonderful food, but someone must kill the animal, grind the meat, stuff it into wrappers, and get it to market in a timely fashion. Making sausage is tough and involves way more than simply coming up with the idea of eating ground meat.

Likewise, commercialization of ideas is hard work. Launching successful innovations is a complete process of coming up with an idea AND launching it. The front end is the fun, creative part of innovation, and the back end is well . . . the back end. The attractiveness of the front end and the ugliness of the back end can prove a detriment to innovation because organizations and their people would rather glamorize the innovations than do the work in the trenches to make them successful. The shiny object syndrome remains a fierce impediment to overcoming Victory Disease.

Two Greats That Led the Way

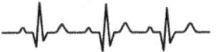

"You can't solve a problem on the same level that it was created. You have to rise above it to the next level."

—Albert Einstein

CHAPTER 32

Alexander the Great:

Historical Example of Overcoming Victory Disease

History is chock-full of noteworthy examples of leaders overcoming Victory Disease to achieve dramatic results. As "lions" in leadership in this regard, Alexander the Great and the Greek expansion fought against complacency and routine to achieve world dominance.

The Macedonians under Alexander the Great were the most creative and innovative military of their era. They conquered a vast portion of the world. Alexander the Great, as their transformational leader, was one of the best military minds in history, a leader who understood the need to innovate and take big risks to achieve big goals. He realized his greatness by innovating from an early age.

Alexander and the Macedonians had every reason to fall victim to Victory Disease. The Macedonians, under Alexander's father, Philip the II of Macedon, had already achieved military greatness through victory after victory. Philip II took the Macedonian crown under very perilous circumstances when the country was under siege and about to collapse. He then used a combination of diplomacy and martial skills to unite the kingdom and fend off the threatening foreign powers. Philip II professionalized the military force and made professional military fighting a way of life for young Macedonian men. Not unlike the Japanese bushido, he inculcated military arts in the Macedonian culture.

Not resting on his laurels, Philip II aggressively moved to subdue and conquer the surrounding territories of the Illyrians, Dardanians, Thracians, and Greeks. He achieved victory after victory while young Alexander learned and watched from his Macedonian palace. Upon Philip's death, Alexander was crowned the new leader at just 20 years old. As the new head of a successful kingdom, the conditions were ripe for Alexander to exude complacency and arrogance. However, young Alexander provided an early formula for overcoming Victory Disease that included constant innovation and prudent, yet aggressive risk-taking. Innovation under Alexander helped the Macedonians become the most successful fighting force on the planet. There are many examples of Alexander's innovation leadership including their fighting model.

They had previously learned to use the Greek phalanx as a fighting model. The phalanx was a formation that allowed them to fight as a tight, well-organized team. It proved far superior to the barbarian's methods of fighting, which relied solely on individual heroism and guts, lacking an emphasis on teamwork. While the barbarians would charge headlong into the fray in a wild, free-for-all frenzy, the Greek phalanxes moved as a single unit, repelling much larger forces. It created a winning model for the Macedonians that had brought much success.

However, Alexander didn't rest on their superiority and thus changed the phalanx formation. The weakness of the phalanx lay in its slow-moving responsiveness. Phalanx units, although able to repel enemies and secure terrain, maneuvered too slow for rapid advancement. Alexander and the Macedonians overcame that weakness by adding a coordinated mobile fighting style, a radical practice for the 4th century BC. They invented the combined-arms model of fighting, adding fast and powerful cavalry units on the flanks of the slow phalanx units. It proved extremely disruptive to the fighting forces of the times. The phalanx units would methodically fight the frontal ranks of their opponents, with the cavalry units then attacking from the flanks. They would break the enemy's ranks and then chase down those scattering, thoroughly defeating them. Its success was so lauded that modifications of this combined arms approach are still used today with tanks and infantry—only Alexander and the Macedonians invented and perfected it 2,300 years ago.

Alexander capitalized on other types of innovation as well—through the use of the latest information and technology to aid their war efforts. In a foreshadowing of what innovators today call *technology transfer*, Alexander and the Macedonians sought out various technologies and strategies to transfer for their use. After hearing of the Sicilians' success in attacking fortresses, Alexander observed the way they strategically maneuvered around forts to avoid direct fire. When he heard of different types of shields in India, he studied and tested those shields, then adopted the best for his use. The Macedonians learned from others' technologies and implemented them for their efforts.

Macedonian listening posts were trained not only to watch for enemy activity, but also to collect and report information about other armies that might prove useful. For example, when the Macedonians learned of superior equipment for sieges, they investigated the technology, studied it for adaptability, and then either produced the new weapons on their own or merely forced the makers to create more for the Macedonian purpose.

Among the many innovations used to achieve success included improved catapults, underground mining to bypass barriers, siege ladders that helped them scale walls, and armored roofs that protected their engineers who worked to bypass or destroy enemy fortresses. All these technology transfers entailed inventions that greatly enhanced Alexander's victories.

Currently, we love to use data for the collection, assessment, and triangulation of information in order to create new solutions and *wow* business experiences. We've even coined the term *big data* to refer to the mass amounts of information we can collect and then transform. Alexander was a master of collecting data and information in his time and using it to support his efforts. When his armies occupied or conquered a new territory, they would gather the various manuscripts and writings for their collection and use. Alexander would use interpreters to translate the documents into the Greek language in order to standardize his collected wisdom and make it more accessible. In this manner, all the accumulated wisdom of his conquests was assembled and used for his future efforts. Whereas most armies of the day pillaged and burned their way through territories, Alexander frequently analyzed and learned. Information was so valued that when a trade or cargo ship entered his port, they were required to provide all manuscripts in their possession. The Macedonians would then make a copy of the books and provide them back to the ship. In this manner, they collected information from all over the world. These manuscripts would later be used to start the library of Alexandria, the most famous library of the ancient world, many of whose books we've preserved to this day.

And you think you were Great? HA!

ALEXANDER MEETS THE COMPUTER

Alexander and the Macedonians also changed how the logistics of war were managed. Typically, if the Greek city-state armies traveled far from home, they took huge baggage trains of non-combatants with them. Before Alexander, senior military officers could travel with large support staffs that treated them like royalty. These extra people included servants carrying armor and supplies, personal slaves, women, and camp followers. This practice often doubled the size of the expedition. When the army deployed, many of the comforts of home went with them. Alexander cut that staff significantly and forced his military leaders to learn to operate in a leaner, more efficient manner.

This change undoubtedly embodied a difficult leadership

move, one that demonstrated Alexander's heightened level of transformational ability. As often happens in modern organizations, the pampered upper levels needed coercing into making uncomfortable change, while the working staff understood the logic and advantages, actually embracing the changes that brought new simplicity. The ranks of Alexander's military leaders were also filled with his former classmates whom he grew up with in the private, affluent schools of Macedonia. His senior commanders were his friends in the aristocracy. And the Macedonia aristocracy, like most aristocracies, was used to tremendous pampering.

Yet Alexander reduced many of their indulgences by cutting the fat. He opted for less opulence in favor of improving logistics. He challenged the status quo. The organization fought him on that change, with some of his senior commanders behaving complacently and disregarding his orders to reduce their footprint. Overcoming those obstacles, Alexander proved decisive; he eliminated the resistant naysayers from his officer ranks in sometimes public and sometimes private removals.

By challenging the status quo, Alexander overcame the culture of complacency and arrogance. And he countered that culture with one of the very best principles of innovation: simplicity. He made simple but effective changes to have each soldier carry his own equipment. The Macedonians also sought to limit the number of large carts taken on war expeditions as they clogged the roads and limited movement. To narrow the people footprint, they reduced the number of support persons and thus maximized the number of fighting force deployed. Alexander became a pioneer in addressing what is called *tooth-to-tail ratio* in modern armies. The *teeth* were the fighting forces, and the *tail* was the logistics and non-fighters. Alexander simplified his army by giving it more teeth and less tail. The result was a fighting force that had a lot of bite. The tooth-to-tail ratio is now routinely used in modern armies to improve combat ratios, but Alexander still stands as one of the innovation pioneers for logistics.

For risk-taking, Alexander became a master of taking prudent, calculated risks. On some of his larger campaigns, he moved across terrain considered completely untraversable and for which no reliable maps existed. So daunting were some of his routes that his enemies didn't bother to defend them; they assumed no armies could cross them. Imagine his risk of moving a large army without knowing for sure where they were going or what hazards might confront them. He took the risks because he knew the rewards were even greater.

And just as compelling, he also did nothing haphazardly. Alexander developed various risk mitigation strategies that helped enhance his uncharted campaigns. He developed advanced scouting techniques and ingenious ways of recruiting locals who knew the routes. Alexander, like all great innovators, used the knowledge of others to connect the dots and bridge the gaps in his information.

Not limited to military solutions, Alexander used political means to influence change. He trained his Macedonian leaders to use diplomacy to gain the support of towns along the routes so the townspeople could aide and advance the solution of supporting the armies. Those towns that chose to ally with them were spared violent takeovers and were assimilated. But those towns that refused support were assaulted and enslaved as an example to others in the area. The result was to encourage villages and townships along the route to play a part in the Macedonian effort and, ultimately, to aid Alexander in moving quickly as he garnered food and supplies from new local allies.

Refusing to rest on his laurels, Alexander the Great assumed risk as a leader to achieve world-class results. The result: Alexander conquered the mighty Persian empire in less than ten years; he opened lasting communications and trade routes between the East and West; and he created functioning civil governments as he moved across the land, building his empire. Using innovative methods, tools, and fighting models, he conquered and subdued two-thirds of the free world. Historians frequently write that Alexander wept when he had no more lands to conquer; yet at 32 years of age, he had not only achieved massive, unprecedented success, but also conquered Victory Disease.

CHAPTER 33

Christopher Columbus: Assuming Entrepreneurial Risk

Christopher Columbus was another historical leader who took tremendous risks in his voyages of discovery. Columbus sought land and sea routes in directions that no one else would go. In a situation not unlike young entrepreneurs seeking angel investments today, Columbus had to find borrowed money and resources from powerful aristocrats who demanded riches in exchange for their support. While the lens of history shows us that the risk paid off (and that others had already proceeded him), his endeavor was terrifying to most normal people of the time. Columbus had acquired the classic *innovation bug*, willing to move in the opposite direction from everyone else. And in his quest to find alternate trade routes to Asia, he wanted to travel into areas where many people still thought the earth fell off into space.

Because Columbus was a risk-taker, he planned to prove his theory through discovery. According to his calculations, an easier, alternate route to the Indies simply had to exist—traveling west, across the Atlantic Ocean. Columbus needed ships and a crew to prove his theory, so he sought venture capital from various monarchies. Columbus' idea was rejected by most rulers: Italy, Portugal, and France all refused his requests. Like most successful entrepreneurs of today, he didn't give up after being told no. After each failed attempt, Columbus regrouped and made plans to target the next potential backer. He finally found an ally in the Queen of Spain, who was willing to take a chance for quicker access to Chinese trade routes.

EARTH SHAPE REGISTRATION

NEXT!

Columbus built his small fleet based on borrowed resources from the Queen, then took a journey into an area that many still felt was off the edge of the earth. It takes a tremendous amount of personal resolve to continue with an idea that other authorities say is impossible. Although his estimates were off, he still discovered new land. As is the case with many innovation mistakes, his mistaken estimates resulted in a new discovery of the Americas. Columbus made three more successive voyages to the Americas before it was over, and in doing so, solidified European expansion to North America. Columbus wasn't complacent about seeking new routes, and in the process, he rediscovered a continent.

Courage and Culture

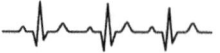

"When the winds of change blow, some people build walls and others build windmills."
—Ancient Chinese proverb

CHAPTER 34

Don't Kill the Messenger (or the Innovator)

Championing innovation and change in an established organization is a rough business. As Victory Disease infects an organization, it promotes the persecution of change agents and makes the role of innovators dangerous. After all, change agents are so termed because they are introducing and implementing change, all a source of pain for the status quo keepers. Just as a diseased body's immune system will sometimes wrongly fight off the very things that provide a cure, so an organization under the throes of Victory Disease will sometimes attack and eliminate their critical change agents.

In my consulting practice, many of my clients have had some sort of bad experience with an innovation effort; and more times than not, the innovators were fired or left the organization. The causes and excuses for these firings have one trait in common— the organization always feels the innovators pose a threat and thus are justified in eliminating them. They are never willing to acknowledge that the reason the innovators are gone is due to a problem within their culture or their leadership. In sick organizations, the innovators gain a reputation as troublemakers— and when that perception is permeated across the culture, the innovators are persecuted.

But innovators and internal entrepreneurs aren't really trouble-makers. They are not the malignant cells that the organism needs to deploy antibodies to kill. Quite the opposite. They are actually caring people who see things differently from the status quo. They are actually the good kind of cells that heal the living tissue of the organization. I usually find that just about 5 percent of an organization's employees fall into the entrepreneurial/innovation type. The *entrepreneurial type* describes a person who seeks solutions that lie outside the organization's mainstream thinking. Even though small in number, they can—if mobilized—become a powerful internal immune system for the organization. Depending on the status of an organization's health, those internal innovators will either already be active in organizational innovation or be somewhere in hiding. Since I am usually called in after the failed attempts at change, I typically find the latter: the natural innovators are hiding in the midst of a sickly organization. While they may still see change opportunities around them, the organization's hostile environment toward that change has trained them to keep their heads down.

For example, one of my large insurance clients hired me to help after their second attempt to launch an innovation program had failed. They wanted me to bring my practical experience to help them succeed as they tried a third time. This particular company saw the changing market and emerging threats but couldn't launch successful initiatives on their own. Because they were a large Fortune 100 company, they had found it easy during their second failed attempt to make a substantial commitment to the effort: five dedicated persons and about $10M dollars.

But even so, their internal innovation team barely lasted two years. Almost immediately after standing them up, the organization started knocking them down—through varied kinds of assaults. These rounds of attacks came in the form of leaders who felt the innovators' work was redundant to other efforts. Some leaders wanted no overlap between the innovators' efforts and theirs. Other leaders felt like the team's effort wasn't the right type of innovation. Since as many definitions of innovation exist as there are people, this criticism was a "gotcha" that the team couldn't overcome. One senior leader told me he felt like the innovation team should have focused on incremental innovation since their company was behind on the basic digitization of their company. He wanted website and app improvements. Another leader told me she didn't want any help with the basic online work, that she had wanted "five years out" revolutionary efforts. Both had good points, but the leaders' expectations didn't align to give the fledgling innovation team any focus and thus left them in a perpetual seesaw state of not knowing what types of innovation to pursue. All the while, they received criticism from whatever senior leader their efforts weren't supporting.

In addition, most employees in this same company self-described the culture as risk-averse, which simply didn't allow any injects of risky or unplanned projects into the system. So, the innovation team really had no way to accomplish anything other than find ideas and propose them to a bureaucracy and leadership team that weren't going to agree on any movement forward.

Under these circumstances, the innovation team was lucky to last two years. They weren't perfect, but their work certainly didn't merit their instantaneous firing. I diagnosed the root cause of the problem at this large insurance company as the underlying arrogance and risk-averse bureaucracy. I had to start my project by telling them the hard truth: their own arrogance and bureaucracy were the cause of the innovation problems. They had to understand that to first heal from Victory Disease, an organization must accept that they have a problem.

Organizational self-destruction happens all too often—and is one of the reasons I've been running a busy innovation practice for a few years. Those organizations needing innovation the most often lack the ability to build a repeatable innovation capability. They don't understand what it takes to launch new ideas in a rigid, risk-averse environment. Their standard procedure is to throw money and people at the problem and assume it will work. While providing resources signifies a good start, a sharp focus, strategic alignment, and the appropriate tactics must follow, which most organizations don't know how to accomplish for innovation. Also, for big change to work, the culture must be massaged and kneaded. If not, when innovation initiatives cause friction within the organization, the culture's knee-jerk response is to fire the innovators (or threaten them in bathrooms).

CHAPTER 35

Military Digitization: Recent Example of Overcoming Victory Disease

A more recent military example lies in the digitization and transformation of the U.S. military that occurred in the late 20th through early 21st centuries. As an Army transformation officer at the time, I was a small part of those efforts and witnessed first-hand the powerful impact of organizational change. At the end of the Cold War, the U.S. military was atop the world as the only superpower. They easily could have rested on their laurels and stopped progressing. But instead of relaxing, they embarked on some of the most significant initiatives in recent history to transform themselves to best-in-class. The U.S. Army developed rapid advancements in global positioning systems, digitization, and night-time vision capabilities; and they deployed them in a manner that transformed the way wars are fought.

Global positioning systems revolutionized military operations as well as spawned many modern disruptive businesses. The Department of Defense initiated the GPS system to improve the navigation systems of warfare and for increased accuracy of missile systems and bombers. Like many innovations do, GPS connects the dots between different inventions, hoping to create combined technologies with greater capability.

Although very expensive at first, the rapid advancements in GPS capabilities were also wildly successful. GPS allowed direct and accurate positioning of aircraft and troops. Previously, commanders at all levels used radio transmissions for determining locations. Radio was an incredible development of its time, but the use of GPS created a whole new paradigm for geolocating. GPS enabled numerous military innovations, including the digitization of the U.S. armed forces, before anyone else. Many modern companies are in the process of digitizing their operations, which usually means making their products and services available in multiple channels such as phone, tablet, and web. For the U.S. military in the '80s and '90s, digitization involved creating an informed network of troops, equipment, and battlefields.

Because of GPS and digitization, military commanders could make informed and accurate decisions that cut through the fog of war. Where previously commanders were limited to radio communications to determine the locations of forces, digitization allowed for a real-time and accurate picture of the battlefield. The old way of determining locations entailed units reporting their locations and then the higher headquarters plotting those locations on a map. The individual reported to the team, the team reported to the squad, the squad reported to the platoon, and on up the reports went—with each level potentially allowing more error into the reports. The system was fraught with problems including miscommunications and location plotting errors. Most egregious was the need to stop fighting in order to report locations. Also, as the number of people that one could report to proved limited, other units might be out of the information loop. Fratricide, the often-tragic scenario of when friendly forces fire upon each other, was ever-prevalent, and the fog of war was present in command and control. Mistakes frequently cost the lives of friendly forces. Thankfully, digitization improved all that.

Digitization allowed military units to focus on their missions while having their positions reported in real-time. Suddenly, military commanders across the battlefield could have a "common operating picture" of all friendly forces—their movements, speeds, and directions. Digitization enabled an accurate depiction on a real-time map of exactly where all units were located. Leaders and field commanders were no longer forced to stop operations and report, then re-report, and then troubleshoot discrepancies. Digitization gave everyone a common map from which they could work. Battlefield synchronization was enhanced a thousand times and gave the U.S. military a competitive advantage. Whereas enemies of the U.S. were still limited to cobbling together a confused mix of radio transmissions to understand the battlefield, the U.S. military could immediately see where units were located, making critical decisions way ahead of their adversaries. Thanks to the innovation of digitization, the U.S. military gained an unfair advantage, which is exactly what you want in war . . . and in business.

GPS was one of the most impactful developments of the last 50 years for navigation and combat operations. And then it became available to the public. In the 1980s, President Ronald Reagan opened the use of GPS for civilian use as a public good. Now, GPS is owned and loosely overseen by the U.S. military as a national resource.

Like so many new inventions, success and new ideas breed more success and new ideas. As soon as GPS was shared with American entrepreneurs, amazing things began to happen. Many of the companies and revolutionary ideas that dominate the landscape today use GPS technology. Companies that I talk about in this book couldn't operate without it. Uber couldn't have disrupted the people transportation industry, UPS and FedEx couldn't have revolutionized the precise delivery of packages, and the mighty Google wouldn't be who they are today without it.

Similar to GPS, night vision capabilities were a game-changing technology in U.S. military operations. Akin to Alexander the Great's ability to lead his armies through unknown places, night vision was a historical first, enabling a military to fight through the darkness.

Night vision started during World War II, but not by the Japanese. The practical night vision devices originated with the Germans for use by both their tanks and infantry. The Americans also developed night vision technologies for use during World War II. Some accounts even exist of Americans using night vision to detect Japanese infantry on Okinawa. However, night vision was not perfected or widely used until the 1980s, when U.S. military transformation got ahold of it. Night vision was then widely distributed, prompting its successful use by the U.S. during the Gulf War in the early 1990s. It gave the U.S. one of its single largest advantages and spawned the somewhat arrogant phrase, "We own the night." Whereas previous armies stopped fighting at night due to the inherent danger and confusion of shooting at unidentifiable things (especially allies) in the dark, during the Gulf War the U.S. military could continue operations long after opposing forces had to stop. The U.S. military therefore doubled the combat time of their efforts—creating a huge advantage.

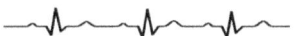

Practical Viewpoint: How a Successful Entrepreneur Thinks

One of the iconic entrepreneurs of our time is Gary Hoover, the founder of the business site Hoover.com and the bookstores Bookstop Inc. (which became Barnes and Noble). While I was the innovation executive at a major U.S. company, I made friends with Gary, who was happy to share his entrepreneurial insight. Gary told me the three questions he asks when looking into a new endeavor:

1) **Am I passionate about the idea or business?** Gary, like so many

entrepreneurs, wants to enjoy what he does. He also knows that building a new business is hard work and thus he must be passionate about the idea to succeed.

2) **Is anyone else doing it or variations of it?** This question is key if you want to disrupt the business space. And while many companies don't need to disrupt the space, sometimes those organizations succumbing to Victory Disease need to think more radically.

3) **Can the idea be successful?** This last question Gary asks is, after all, what an idea is all about. But the success question is not necessarily the only important thing to ask. Many successful organizations think that success is the only factor and ignore the idea's uniqueness and passion. Without uniqueness and passion, businesses that try to innovate sometimes end up merely building a bigger battleship.

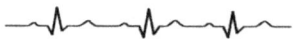

Now, like almost all military innovations, night vision has been adapted for all sorts of commercial uses and industries including transportation and even sport hunting. Presently, almost all militaries employ night vision technologies to enable operations at any time. As with most innovations, the advantages and benefits are eventually adopted by just about everyone.

CHAPTER 36

Creating a Culture of Innovation

Staying true to Einstein's approach, I've mostly focused on the pain and problems of Victory Disease up until now. However, the next two chapters will broadly describe the solutions and remedies available to counteract its spread. And while it's good to understand and accurately diagnose the ailment, we ultimately want to counteract the disease.

If you want to neutralize Victory Disease, addressing organizational culture is a good place to start; *culture* is the single most important factor in finding a cure. The simplest way to define culture is "the way an organization does things." And the way an organization does things needs to be altered and influenced to embrace change and innovation.

Usually a discussion of culture scares people away. The mention of culture suggests an image of anthropologists exploring the far reaches of various foreign countries, analyzing the actions of different peoples. Yet actually, culture in our context describes a complicated matrix of habits, norms, and symbols that shape the actions of an organization. To leaders and innovators, culture might appear as a very large, slow-moving battleship, one out of our control. In the cold and hard business world of profits, the soft science nature of culture appears scary and un-businesslike. The whole topic can seem unmanageable and give the impression it should be avoided at all costs.

Rather than view culture as a scary subject, however, we need to manage it—because culture is the environment in which innovation must thrive. New ideas live or die in the ecosystem in which they are born. Once viewing culture in that light, we must address it. In other words, the culture simply supplies the water, air, and energy in varying amounts to make things happen, to make things grow. If culture is the way an organization does this, the way it does things, then it can and must be understood. And once "the way" an organization operates is understood, then it can be worked with, or worked around, where necessary.

For example, 3M is the master of culture, the paradigm others frequently study to learn about exemplary innovation in successful companies. Although they have seen success for over 100 years and could have easily fallen victim to Victory Disease along the way, they have overcome the symptoms through an environment that rewards their scientists' creativity and risk-taking. I had the opportunity to partner with them and study their culture when I was a large organization innovator.

3M's key was creating a hero culture around innovation that propels everyone to want to innovate. Their leaders tell me their innovation success is founded on their culture. The culture allows for up to 20 percent of employees' time to be spent innovating. When a 3Mer has an idea, they're assured of three things: where to find partners, how to obtain resources, and that they can easily get approval to explore their idea. They embrace institutionalized innovation teamwork through the "two-call" rule, which states that any idea originator should be able to reach the right person to answer their questions within two calls. All this ecosystem support means that ideas with merit gain the opportunity to grow quickly.

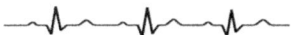

Practical Reflection: People Influence the Culture
The 3M "Technology Forum" was a very successful program that

formalized the ability of employee teams to dedicate time and energy to pursue new ideas. Run by and for employees, it empowered everyone to bring their ideas to fruition. Here's the way it worked: Any employee could have any idea and form a team to pursue that idea. If the employee generated interest in their idea among the team, they were given time and some funding to pursue their idea's development. The program was run very loosely, and structured so approval was easily obtained. A super-innovative employee from the company ranks was appointed and rotated each year to oversee the program.

3M expects approximately 50 percent of their new revenue to come from innovations over a five-year period. While this goal proves remarkable, it's enabled by the culture of innovation that 3M has fostered over the years. Very few 3M employees can tell you the names of the previous 3M CEOs, but most can tell you the name of the inventor of Post-It notes. Innovators are the heroes at 3M, not the "ivory tower" overpaid CEOs. Their type of culture, which recognizes the role of people in innovation, is extremely conducive to creating and launching new ideas and products. Because innovation is "the way they do things" at 3M, both ideas and their creators flourish.

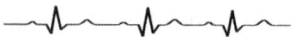

Knowing what the cultural bias entails enables an organization to recognize when an idea runs counter to this bias. This approach allows innovators either to build a different version that capitalizes on the cultural bias or to work around the bias through other techniques.

Because culture is the most critical determinant of how innovation works (or doesn't work), organizations that earnestly want to build an innovation program should begin with a frank assessment of the culture as it relates to innovation. Henry Ford is famous for his comment, "Culture eats strategy for breakfast." And while that undoubtedly holds true, one can equally assert, "Culture eats innovation for lunch." The organization's culture proves so critical that they must address it first before it devours innovation.

A culture assessment is one of the critical projects I complete for my larger clients. They frequently have never thought holistically about how culture affects their innovation. Yet, culture underpins everything and will immediately reflect the presence of any of the ABC symptoms of Victory Disease. While I have 30 years of innovation expertise that helps me with these assessments, anyone at any level can conduct them as long as the organization provides them access. Below is an outline of the methodology I use for my culture assessments.

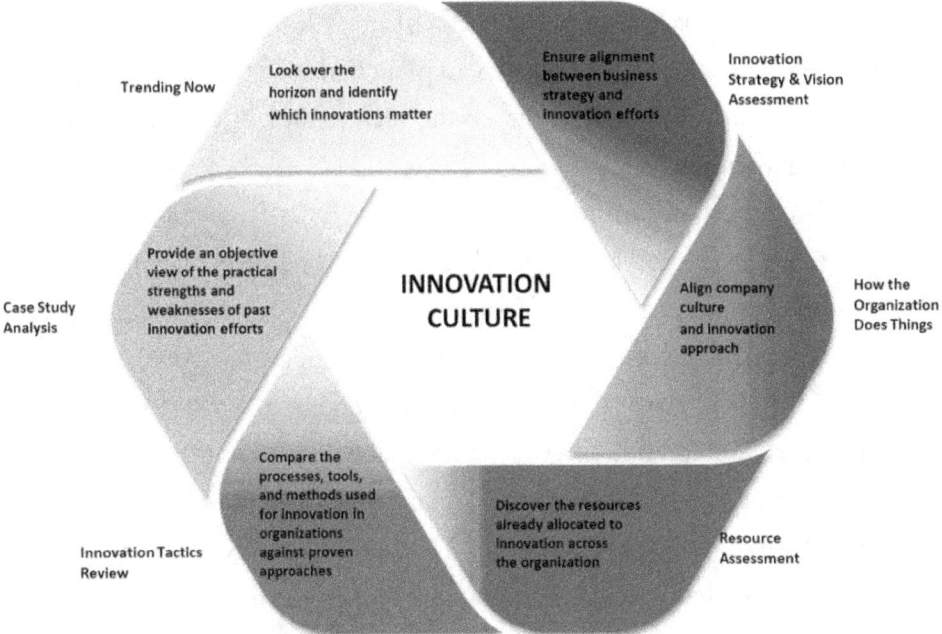

My Assessment Rubrik for Innovation Culture

CHAPTER 37
Ideas Need a Place to Grow

A common early mistake of organizations as they try to overcome their malaise lies in a hyper focus on ideas. I call this focus *the cult of ideas,* whereby generating ideas becomes everything, without actually *launching* any of them. And while ideas are important, the organizational culture in which those ideas need to grow is tantamount. The ideas are the seeds of growth that we all love to see flourish. Like a seed that we can plant and see grow into a large tree that yields delicious fruit, so the idea is the embryo of every great innovation.

But ideas, as important as they are, need the appropriate environment in which to grow. Just as a seed requires water, soil, sunlight, and air in the right doses, a new idea requires the various components of an organizational culture to support its growth. One can't throw a seed onto bare ground and expect it to grow miraculously; and one likewise cannot take an idea and toss it into a meeting room and expect the organization to rally around it. It just doesn't happen that way. This is especially true in an organization that is succumbing to any of the symptoms of Victory Disease.

Victory Disease organizations will be so caught up in their own beliefs about the future that they will ignore and even kill new ideas. The culture will deny the sickness and demand to continue the status quo. Akin to the boisterous toasts of Japanese officers extolling the future victories to come, so a modern organization in the throes of Victory Disease continuously compliments itself. It all seems very right to the people inside the infected organization, but what is really happening is the perpetuation of a model that is being disrupted by changes in the external environment.

As the leader of a large U.S. company innovation program, I was always aware of the symptoms of Victory Disease and felt like we had to constantly battle them to keep their threatening tentacles from pulling us down. The conditions were always ripe for Victory Disease. The company itself was doing very well, achieving or exceeding its goals for the ninety-plus years it had been in existence. No strong reasons arose to embrace change or innovation, particularly because of a strongly loyal customer base. Although the company started as an entrepreneurial endeavor for a group of Army officers who insured each other in a new creative manner, I felt like the company had slipped into the traditional risk aversion that characterizes most successful financial services companies.

Even though very few recognized our burning platform for change, amazing opportunities to innovate were arrayed across the company. Small and large opportunities were evident in every part of the organization. At the start of my tenure leading innovation, the enterprise innovation team pursued ideas with great enthusiasm, anticipating positive results. Expecting the rest of the company to embrace the excitement, the team was disappointed when new idea after new idea was slowed or stopped for one reason or another. The first year our innovation initiative launched a dismal three ideas across the enterprise. The second year we launched only nine ideas. Although we presented numerous great ideas with promising futures, they didn't take hold in the organization. The ideas were either reduced from great ideas to small incremental ones or delayed and killed by bureaucracy.

Although the small program was strongly backed by the CEO and led by motivated innovators, the ideas were fighting against the culture of a large, successful financial services company. The culture was all about maintaining the status quo and preventing disruption to their winning ways, even at the expense of new ideas. We came to the hard realization that innovation wasn't just about developing the ideas; it was about creating a more conducive environment in which the ideas could grow.

We realized we needed to influence the culture of the organization. Previously, the strategic innovation objectives had focused solely on launching new ideas to bring value to customers. Once the role of culture in new ideas was fully accepted, my innovation team developed an equally important objective: to create a mature ecosystem in which innovation could thrive.

We crafted a strategy for shaping the culture and were slowly able to influence key leaders that were in positions to help. We learned that innovation was a team sport, best played out with everyone involved. Among the key leaders needed were human resources professionals, communications people, and business heads.

Human resources, as in many organizations, controlled most of the long-term, culture-shaping objectives that really made a difference. Tasks such as creating and communicating performance objectives, rewards, and hiring practices are critical to the culture-shaping necessary for innovation. Human resource policies determine who is hired into organizations, who is promoted, how people are rewarded, and how they are penalized. We began a campaign that made risk-taking and innovative thinking a key component of hiring and promotion. Instead of only selecting people who had "met the numbers," we could infuse the promotion processes with rewards for people who took risks on new ideas and encouraged change.

The communications team was also very important. Both internal and external communications are the key to spreading the word about innovation. Internally, communications can play an instrumental role in sharing successes and bringing the "banner and balloons" celebrations that helps the innovative spirit to spread. Externally, they can share innovations with customers and shareholders, which indirectly influences the employees.

No matter the size of the organization, business and line leaders always play a critical role. They determine innovation objectives, hiring practices, responses to risk . . . and even how the organization treats failure. Transformational leaders, those who embrace and implement positive change, are critical to innovation success.

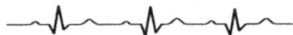

Practical Viewpoint: How to Tell Your Venture Story
—by Dr. Cliff Zintgraff

Has an idea ever been clear in your mind, but then the more you work on it, the less clear it becomes? People and organizations who have prior success often fall slowly into bad habits when it comes to telling the story of their work. Simple stories become complex; well supported claims get exaggerated; clear ideas that flowed one-to-the-next give way to complex narratives. This backsliding is not good! Few things are more fundamentally important to innovators than being able to communicate their stories in quick, simple, and compelling ways.

I've worked with hundreds of ventures, some startups, some non-profits, and some internal to large companies. I've found that a few simple rules can help innovators keep their stories on track, and more importantly, can help them not lose their way as the facts of their case change underneath them (inevitable in any real venture!).

First, keep each idea (each presentation slide, or each verbal point) clear and self-contained. Ideas that do double-duty are generally confusing, and you miss a chance to connect one idea to the next. Stories that begin with a clear and compelling problem statement leave an audience dying to hear the proposed solution! But if the problem is half-stated in a rush to share a "great idea" with the world, the audience winds up confused, and usually less than convinced that a real problem exists.

Second, use conclusions to inspire the next questions. Remember, a great problem statement drives a listener to ask, "how do we fix that?" The question forms in your listener's mind, and then you answer it! Every step along the way is a chance to inspire a question you can answer. Will that proposed solution work? Show them how. Will people actually use this solution? Answer with the voice of customers. Can this make money? Show your audience some details.

Third, no new material facts after the half-way point of your story! A hallmark of a "lost" presentation is the entry of major new technical or market research information being introduced in the final thoughts of a presentation. Almost every time, there was either a failure in prior analysis or the story is losing its focus. Think of the first half of your story as laying the foundation, and the second half as making your case.

Finally, sum up! This is a simple but powerful idea, especially for longer presentation formats. What are the two or three main reasons your argument is a good one? The main reasons it makes sense to take your venture forward? There are two really good reasons to offer a summation. For your audience, it shares and hopefully confirms the main ideas that make your venture go. For you, it forces the argument into a clean landing. Your ability to conclude your argument is a good measure of the consistency of your overall presentation.

For me, telling a story is not something I do myself, even when I present solo. It's a co-creation with the audience. As much as I'm sharing ideas, I want to be inspiring many thoughts. The more I inspire good questions that I turn around and answer, the more persuasive the story of my work. These four rules can help you make, and keep, a powerful narrative about why you're creating something new.

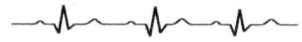

CHAPTER 38
Transformational Leadership Is Essential

Pulitzer Prize-winning author James Burns first introduced the concept of transformational leadership in his 1978 book, *Leadership*.[17] Burns distinguished between two types of leaders: transactional and transformational. He defined a transactional leader as someone focused on the role of supervision, organization, and group performance; and inversely, he described a transformational leader as someone more focused on boosting team motivation, morale, and performance. He posited that "transformational leadership occurs when one or more persons engage with others in such a way that leaders and followers raise one another to higher levels of motivation and morale."

Unfortunately, many of today's successful organizations are not led by transformational but by transactional leaders, those who lead from behind in an autocratic and efficient manner. But today's fast-moving world is better suited for the transformational type—leaders who are nimble, involved, and committed to recognizing and inspiring the individuals within their organization.

Long before Burns, Austrian American economist Joseph Schumpeter shared a similar view on leadership styles. He identified innovation as the critical dimension of economic change, arguing that innovation and technological change must come from entrepreneurs or, as he termed them, *wild spirits*. Schumpeter coined the terms *entrepreneur-spirit* and *creative destruction* to assert that individual entrepreneurial types are the agents that drive innovation. He said that if employed within large companies, they are more capable of making a significant difference because these companies have the required resources and capital to invest in the best ideas.

Transformational leaders intellectually stimulate their organizations and challenge the status quo, but more importantly, they encourage their team members to challenge the status quo as well. They create an environment in which it is acceptable for individuals to openly share ideas and question traditional ways of doing business. This, in turn, fosters organization-wide innovation.

So, if transformational leaders can be recruited and identified in the ranks, it stands to reason that successful organizations stand a greater chance of being able to take advantage of emerging business models, technological advances, and so on. To make this happen, companies must aim to foster and develop transformational leaders from within. They must also go beyond simply identifying knowledge, skills, and abilities to look for the specific traits that make a transformational leader when hiring externally. Transformational leadership proves a powerful antidote to Victory Disease.

It's worth noting, however, that transformational leadership and transactional skills are not mutually exclusive. Organizations must, of course, focus on staying in business, and this requires current operations to run in an organized and efficient manner. In a consumer lending firm, for example, innovation may help to grow the business, but if its leaders aren't focused on the complexities of regulation, they will quickly find themselves facing fines and even insolvency. In fact, without embracing some aspects of transactional leadership, it's likely that successful organizations will not have the stability required to plunge capital into new ventures. Obtaining the right mix of attributes in a leadership team remains crucial, with most leadership needing more transformational thinking.

Because rapid change is now part and parcel of today's business environment, and is continuing to accelerate, old markets are shifting while new markets are created. *Creative destruction* is presenting both threats and opportunities to successful institutions. Organizations that die will be the ones that fail to recognize their symptoms. If they are risk-averse or unable to transform quickly enough, they will lose market share to their more flexible and agile competitors. Those that embrace change, however, have vast opportunities before them.

Many established organizations already have the intellectual and business capital to take advantage of the changing environment—and should be able to transform their existing lines of business into even more lucrative ventures. What they are missing are ambidextrous leaders who can simultaneously run the day-to-day operations of the business and strategically transform the business to new heights. In this era of hyper-innovation, organizations must identify and embrace their transformational leaders to take them forward—it's a matter of survival.

Major innovations require risk-taking. There is no way around it. Innovation is inherently risky, and the more innovative the idea, the more risk involved. There are lots of ways to mitigate risk and fail fast and cheaply. But no matter the precautions and methods taken, risk can never be fully eliminated. In my twenty-five-plus years of innovation efforts, I've only successfully launched a small handful of those attempted, probably less than 5 percent. That means 95 percent of the innovations failed, and that most of our innovation attempts didn't pay off. However, the 5 percent that did succeed more than made up for the losses of the others. In fact, innovation at my organizations and with my clients brought a huge competitive advantage. But failure and risk are also part of the equation and must be accepted. Successful innovations and their resulting advantages will never come about without transformational leaders and innovators who accept and learn from failure.

Leaders are feeling the pressure to take risks now more than ever. Innovation is in hyper-drive around the world. Successful organizations are made small when their ideas become stale, and startup organizations grow rapidly when their ideas create new markets. Small companies become giant companies when their ideas are fresh and innovative. Behind all the successes are leaders who boldly pursue new ideas, and behind all the dying companies are leaders who sheepishly avoid the risk. And now that the world spins in a historic period of unprecedented innovation and change, that potential requires leaders with courage and the ability to overcome risk.

Glofish

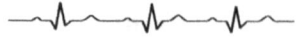

Practical Viewpoint: Technology Transfer Is Everywhere,
like in Glofish®

My friends at the Innovation, Creativity, and Capital Institute in Austin,

Texas, empower college students to learn technology transfer in order to spawn new ideas. Glofish® are one such amazing innovation that has come out of their program to disrupt a once static and complacent market. The pet fish market was about as static as one can get. After all, pet fish are fish, and not much has changed in the ornamental fish market. Not much, until . . . Glofish.

Glofish are certain species of tank fish that glow in the water. The appeal of tank fish has always been aesthetic, but now glowing fish have added an entirely new uniqueness to aquarium fish. Using technology transfer, the founders of Glofish LLC found some scientists at the National University of Singapore who had genetically modified a zebrafish to become fluorescent. They purchased the rights to the new glowing fish, applied entrepreneurial principles to build a business model, and started a run to transform the pet fish market. Now, Glofish are one of the best-selling aquarium fish in the U.S., and Glofish LLC has taken a large market share from the standard run-of-the-mill aquarium suppliers—and all in a market once considered static.

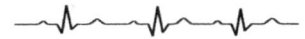

CHAPTER 39
Assuming Risk

The conventional avoidance of risk is strong in successful companies. This statement is true because most leaders have risen through the ranks while learning to focus on incremental revenue growth and cost reductions. The art of *taking* risk has mostly been replaced with the skill of *eliminating* risk. Like the Japanese in World War II, many leaders prefer to build the next iteration of the current battleship. And while most leaders are happy to talk about innovation and even use the current buzzwords to talk the talk, very few are willing to walk the walk. Only a small minority of senior leaders are consistently talking and walking as true change agents.

A recent (short) engagement of mine with a mid-size financial service company illustrates the point. The company wanted to improve their innovation program and launch more impactful innovations, so they hired me to help. Almost immediately I noticed they lacked a vision or goal to raise aspirations for their innovations, and therefore, they lacked clear objectives to support a vision. During the initial interviews, senior leaders of the company each deferred the innovation vision and objectives to someone else. Due to the fear of failure, no one was willing to put a stake in the ground for what they wanted to accomplish. If they took no risks, no one could hold them responsible for any failures. Complacency and fear of failure were present and visible. In a war environment, this scenario would be called cowardice. Finally, the CEO, whom most of the other leaders said had to be the visionary, agreed to an interview.

NO RISK, NO REWARD!

WRIGHT BROS. FARM

Since this company was very hierarchical in structure and decision-making, the CEO was probably the best source for the innovation vision. He needed to be their Alexander or Columbus and assume the risk. Unfortunately, the CEO immediately maneuvered around the idea of innovation vision and objectives. He said any bold vision had to come from somewhere else because he was feeling pressure from some very aggressive board-directed goals. The CEO (who was earning a healthy ~$20M annually) stated, "I'm not in a position to take chances." I reasoned with him and suggested that innovation would ultimately help him achieve and exceed his goals. He tacitly agreed, but then asked me to be the one to come up with, and socialize, *my* vision. It became clear that the leadership team was afraid to lead innovation, with the CEO the most fearful of all. Therefore, the company's intentions for positive change were floating rudderless. I saw that no one would assume responsibility or take accountability for the success of innovation within the organization. My engagement ended after the interviews, and the company has not launched any major products or services in the two years since.

Conversely, a smaller number of organizations exist that have very courageous senior leaders, those who see the benefits of taking risk and know their role includes overcoming fear. They usually lead their companies to greater heights. I witnessed one such leader of a mid-size banking organization use his actions as a positive example to show his company how to behave. The leaders in his organization, as in the previous example, were afraid to act. The CEO, recognizing their fear, led the charge for innovation. He personally sponsored a major innovation challenge and then used his position as CEO to provide updates to the organization on the outcomes. When some of the ideas failed, he stood up at an executive meeting and explained the failure, and then described what he and the team had learned from it. The response from his executives was amazing as his leaders realized that failure was allowed in the pursuit of positive change. During the next set of innovation challenges, almost every C-suite executive volunteered to sponsor an effort. It sent a powerful message to the risk-averse leaders and gave a shot in the arm against Victory Disease. The Romans' Latin phrase "Audentes fortuna iuvat" (Fortune favors the bold) applies just as much to business as it does to war.

The bold leaders willing to take risks are the ones who will realize the benefits of innovation. Buzz words don't launch innovations—gutsy leaders willing to take calculated risks are the ones that do. Transformational leaders bring exceedingly great value to their organizations and customers.

CHAPTER 40

The Magic Elixir—People

People's roles in organizations have changed dramatically, and to recover from Victory Disease, companies must understand and embrace these changes. Employees, partners, and customers are now the most critical components to new growth. Innovation is a people business, where collaboration and teamwork are paramount. The days of crazy inventors working alone in isolated rooms have been usurped by powerful ways for normal people to crowdsource and co-create ideas. Additionally, the new younger generations readily embrace change and are perfect fits for the initiatives needed to overcome Victory Disease. People are the key component of the antidote, and the good news is that most of them want to help.

Organizations are always asking, "What traits does the right person need in order to lead an innovation effort with an established organization?" In response, my former research partner Celent and I asked innovation leaders currently immersed in those leadership capacities what they thought were the required skills. These leaders included those currently heading innovation in successful organizations. Their responses are detailed below:

Charts 1-3: Desired Innovation Skills *(higher is better)*

Personal Attributes - All Industries

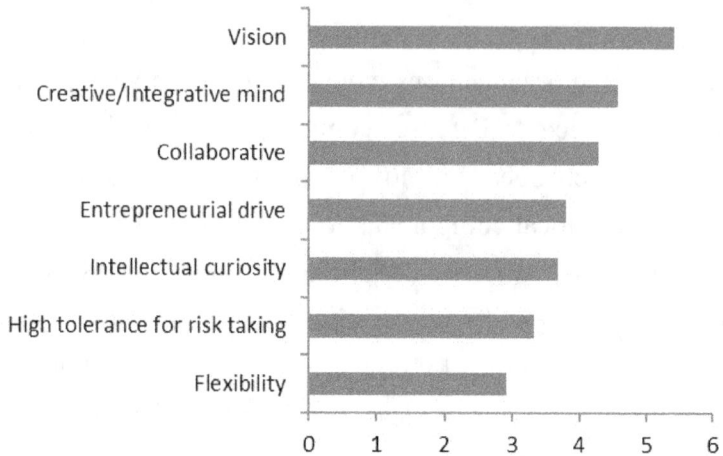

Leadership Qualities - All Industries

Technical Skills - All Industries

Organizational Antidotes
for Victory Disease

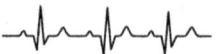

"Never tell people how to do things. Tell them
what to do and they will surprise you with their
ingenuity."

General George Patton

CHAPTER 41
Where Art Meets Science

Reversing the impact of Victory Disease is both an art and a science. The art side of the effort is knowing and understanding the biases and culture of the organization and working within the culture to effect positive and lasting change. The science of the effort is using innovation tactics and techniques to achieve the strategic objectives of the organization. Using the programs for maximum effect is science, but knowing which programs to use and how to use them is more of an art. The good news is that programmatic cures are at hand.

I usually group innovation efforts under the seven major methods listed below. I love it when an organization is serious and committed to change and tries everything at once, but most organizations are not prepared for that and better suited to select one or two methods, and then grow their way into a more dynamic innovation approach. You can group many methods and techniques in multiple ways, but the basic seven methods I use include the following:

- Internal innovation teams
- Crowdsourcing
- Innovation labs or Skunk works®
- Partnerships
- Accelerator or incubation memberships
- Corporate venture capital
- Mergers and acquisitions

Each of these methods has its pros and cons, and they work better or worse depending on the organization and its many variables. The following chapters summarize each method and how it can be employed to fight the effects of Victory Disease.

CHAPTER 42
Internal Innovation Teams

Of the seven cures for Victory Disease, one of the most frequently used is *internal innovation teams*. These teams are dedicated people employed to specifically promote the innovation efforts within the organization. The teams can be as small as one person or as large as 10,000. They can be cross-functional or all focused on the same internal business unit. Organic, internal teams are called different things, such as innovation, research and development, strategic initiatives, transformation, or any other names that suit the organizational environment.

Internal innovation teams often comprise the first line of fire or method used toward fighting Victory Disease. They are sometimes staffed with organizational insiders, and other times with outsiders—both have their benefits. The benefits of insiders filling the team is that they have the immediate ability to navigate the organization's traps. An insider will know who the power brokers are, what steps to take for approvals, and the remaining bureaucratic minefields that await an initiative. The benefit of an outsider team leading innovation lies in the fact they aren't burdened with the way the organization has always done it. The old business model with all the old problems aren't part of their history, so they are much less affected by taking them on. When I help build a client's innovation team, I initially prefer to hire most of the team from within the organization so they don't have the additional early struggle of learning the organization's ropes and subtle nuances. As the internal innovation team grows and progresses, I then seek external help for some of their functions, as an outside perspective proves refreshing and needed.

Some organizations immediately seek an external entrepreneur (sometimes called *intrapreneur*) to lead their organization. Yet, those folks usually end up frustrated and confused by the organization's bureaucracy. Entrepreneurial success in developing a small company from startup to profitability is very different from growing new initiatives in an already successful organization. My experience in consulting has taught me that intrapreneurs brought into the early stages of a program become punching bags for the bureaucracy until they get beat up so much, they go elsewhere. A better early choice for internal innovation is a battle-hardened internal executive who also has the innovative spirit and a reputation for embracing risk and change. This preference was echoed by my research partners Celent and our research shown below on what job experience proved most valuable for an internal innovation leader. *Previous innovation leadership* and *business expertise* were numbers one and two, respectively. When I followed up with some of the respondents, they said those rankings resulted because the speed and difficulty of the endeavor would surprise someone without prior experience.

Chart 4: Desired Job Experience Skill *(higher is better)*

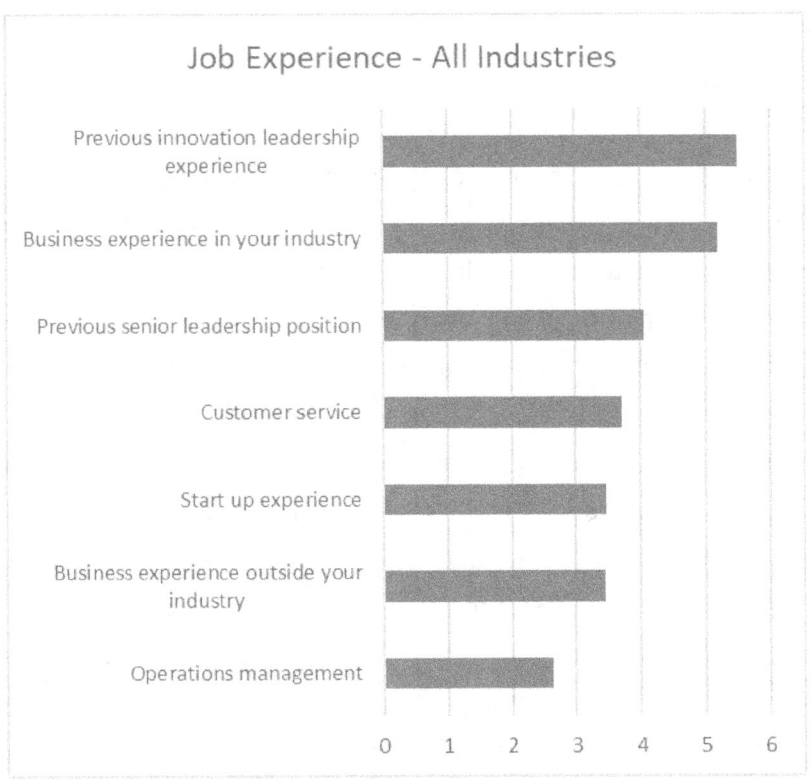

Job Experience - All Industries

More than half of my clients within the financial services industry have some sort of internal organization team, the most commonly used method for innovation. Organizations are used to the structure and understand the need to have some sort of organic innovation center. The largest downside in these internal teams lies in the frequency they are under-resourced and not tied into the organization's fiber. This causes some teams to become irrelevant. Nonetheless, internal teams remain a starting point for organizations to begin their path to new solutions.

CHAPTER 43
Crowdsourcing

Another potential cure to Victory Disease lies in *crowdsourcing*, a term that simply means using larger, more diverse populations to obtain information or ideas that benefit the organization. Crowdsourcing can be internal to an organization's own employees, external to outside communities, or a combination of both. Crowdsourcing enables users to propose ideas or make suggestions, and for others to support or refute the ideas. The goal is to develop a better pipeline of ideas by involving the wisdom of the crowd. In my experience, crowdsourcing is best utilized to solve specific business problems or challenges, as opposed to open-ended "give us your ideas" types of campaigns. There are many pros to crowdsourcing. It is usually inexpensive; after all, ideas are cheap, and people are usually happy to give them to you if you ask them and appreciate their input. Internal crowdsourcing is also a great way to involve and empower the organizational workforce. And it can bypass normal, hierarchical chains of command to jump-start ideation.

The major downsides of crowdsourcing include follow-through on the back end of innovation and the quality of the ideas. The follow-through for launching ideas often emerges weak. Here's the way it works: a campaign is launched to generate ideas, a lot of attention is devoted to collecting ideas, and then the best ideas are selected. The issue becomes who will sponsor and fund an idea, and how it will get launched. After the hullabaloo of the campaign, the selected ideas frequently get stuck in no-man's land because the ideas were not nested within the organization's strategic plan. The organization has a plan, developed by the leadership, that is backed with resources. Yet the new ideas from crowdsourcing are not part of that plan. The contributors then become frustrated trying to enter into the resourcing process. This can have an adverse effect on the community, signaling them that the organization isn't serious about change but merely using innovation as a marketing or employee engagement ploy. The solution for this frequently occurring problem is to establish the resourcing and sponsorship before the challenge even begins, and to obtain commitment from the appropriate organizational leaders to launch the new ideas.

The other major problem with crowdsourcing lies in the quality of ideas. The crowdsourcing platforms and companies will not disclose this, but most of the ideas from internal crowdsourcing will consist of smaller, incremental ideas. You usually won't describe ideas originating from employees and customers as hugely transformational; but when they are, the crowd is likely to shoot them down. Smaller, ankle-biter ideas are usually the best for a crowd.

While leading innovation at a large company, one of our best big idea guys would place his big ideas on our crowdsourcing site. And while we had tremendous success with very small ideas that brought incremental value, with participation of upwards of 90 percent of our total employees, the disruptive ideas that the big idea person presented were frequently voted down by the mass of participants as unfeasible. This was the very same ideator who would be part of some of our biggest technological innovations processed through my innovation team. Yet, his ideas were killed by the crowd.

When I had the "biggest failures" quarterly lunch meeting wherein I met with those crowdsourcing employees whose ideas received the largest negative score, our big idea person was usually in the group. This wasn't because his ideas were bad; they were sometimes great. They just weren't the types of ideas that an internal crowd could wrap their heads around, and so the crowd didn't vote them up. Or sometimes his ideas could impact the crowds' jobs—a hard hurdle to overcome as most people understandably can't support an idea that might potentially axe their position. Internal crowdsourcing is just not conducive for big, disruptive ideas.

Organizations that have a big idea employee or want transformational ideas will need to use one of the other methods for promoting innovation. Transformational ideas get killed by internal crowdsourcing, but it can be very good for small, well-known problems or for front-line problems where the crowd has some expertise.

External crowdsourcing is a bit different in that it uses external crowds for ideation, and it can definitely be used for bigger ideas. External crowdsourcing works the same as the internal kind but uses external people to contribute. Those people do not have to be affiliated with the organization in any way and may even be international. The diversity of the external crowd differentiates it from internal crowd-sourcers, who are usually very familiar with the organization. External crowd-sourcers are more independent in their thinking.

Some organizations see great success with external crowdsourcing while others flop. One of the best practices for external crowdsourcing lies in using it to find solutions to a very specific question or challenge. Another useful way to approach external crowdsourcing is to structure the challenge so the organization seeking solutions only pays when a satisfactory innovation is provided. That way, the farm isn't sold seeking solutions from Timbuktu.

CHAPTER 44
Innovation/R&D Labs

Innovation/R&D labs or skunkworks may be considered a form of internal innovation, but I look at them separately because laboratories possess some characteristics that set them apart. An innovation lab is a semi-autonomous organization that uses a variety of participants to make and build ideas and businesses. They can also use experimental or quasi-experimental methods to test their new ideas. In this sense, one could consider skunkworks, as used during World War II, as a lab of sorts.

Skunkworks differ from the normal innovation lab in that they tend to be more separate from the organization to allow the more transformational ideas to develop, unaffected by the rest of the organization. Labs and skunkworks are particularly effective at building solutions that require cross-functional expertise because the structure allows various skillsets to be brought in from both inside and outside the organization. A myriad of benefits also come with this structure. Labs and skunkworks can build things that are ready for launch; they help with the most difficult part of launching new innovations, the back end.

The major downside to innovation/R&D labs offers a bit of a double-edged sword. Because by nature they are separated from the organization to increase their effectiveness, this same separation so critical to get ideas rolling can also prevent the organization from adopting and implementing them. The real challenge then becomes how to integrate their more disruptive prototypes and ideas into the fabric of the organization. The more separated the development process and the more radical the idea, the more difficult it becomes to integrate the idea into the organization's operations. Agile development methods cross the gap to merge labs into the launch process. Agile processes, however, are most useful for incremental ideas. Successful organizations have pre-existing processes and ways they operate, which center around their business operations. Labs and skunkworks sometimes operate outside those processes, and thus their more revolutionary ideas frequently run into friction as they try to gain a foothold within the organization.

Some considerable research exists showing that new ideas must have a connection to both the strategy and operational expertise of the mother organization or else they don't integrate well. If either the operational expertise or strategic linkage aren't present in the new venture, the innovation has a hard time gaining traction in the organizational mechanics. Innovation lab projects are notorious for developing great revolutionary ideas that the organization rejects. For that reason, I counsel my clients that new ideas that are distinct from the current strategy or expertise of the organization must have new avenues opened for them, in the form of either new lines of business or distinct and separate new organizations. If organizations don't build the correct structure to fit their lab or skunkworks ideas, all their innovative efforts will live up to their name. The funny smell coming from their building may be their festering, unimplemented ideas.

CHAPTER 45
Partnerships

Partnerships provide a fantastic method for new ideas and ventures to take flight that can also heal Victory Disease. By *partnership* I am referring to a true partnership whereby two or more organizations work together for a common goal, with each sharing their expertise and learning from the other's expert capabilities. I am not talking about client/vendor relationships whereby someone merely sells something to someone else. Frequently, organizations demonstrating arrogance will treat potential partners as vendors and be unable to truly partner—that's not the partnership I am referencing (or that is needed).

The best partnerships are symbiotic relationships in which the partners each bring something to the endeavor that the other lacks or needs. The organizations are open and sharing, with each able to share their vulnerabilities and weaknesses with the other; ideally, they also fill each other's innovation needs around one or more specific business challenges.

Partnerships can offer a great way to build innovation because they supplement an organization's capabilities with someone else's—creating something better than the summation of them both left alone. In great partnerships, one plus one equals two . . . million.

An example of a successful fast-food innovative partnership is the Doritos and Taco Bell brand partnership that created the Doritos Locos Taco. Borne from both Doritos and Taco Bell R&D, the Locos Taco surpassed the one-billion-dollar mark for sales in just two years.[18] The success wasn't just the idea—that's the easy part. It was in the partnership teams working through all the issues and challenges to find a solution that *wowed* the customer.

The idea was good, but the partnership allowed the Doritos and Taco Bell teams to experiment with new solutions. They figured out how to combine two great products to create an even greater one. They had to overcome several challenges: the brittleness of the Doritos versus the strength needed for a taco shell; the necessity for the flavor profiles to match; and the fact that the nacho cheese had to really taste like Doritos Nacho Cheese chips. Both teams did what a great partnership does and complemented each other to create a greater result. As a result, the Doritos Loco Taco became the number one product for Taco Bell and has spawned numerous other spinoff products. A good partnership like this combines the best of both organizations to create something even better—an excellent way to innovate.

But partnerships in general do have to take many risks, which are well documented. One of the major risks of innovation partnerships lies in the inability of successful organizations to let their guard down to truly partner with someone (just like in dating relationships). All partners must be willing to expose their soft underbelly and share their weaknesses and their strengths. Then, after achieving success, the partners must not get greedy; each must be willing to share their success with their counterpart.

This outcome is easier said than done for successful organizations, especially arrogant ones. They are used to acting as the 800-pound gorilla, placing demands on others and not having to be vulnerable or open. But this kind of egotistical behavior will not result in achieving anything groundbreaking because the partners don't see themselves as equal and won't have equal incentives to participate. Inevitably when partnerships fail, the cause is due to one or both organizations treating each other as "vendors" instead of partners.

The key here is equality. A vendor is merely an organization from which something is acquired in a temporary manner. There isn't two-way sharing or a truly collaborative approach. One organization makes demands on the other organization (the vendor) to produce a result. Partnership attempts frequently fail when the partnership descends into a vendor relationship. Bad partnerships are characterized by distrust, demands, and red-lined contracts. When lawyers begin playing a larger role in partnerships than do creativity and innovators, then partnerships fail.

While I was on the Notre Dame Innovation Board, we used a powerful partnership method to dislodge diseased thinking and get leaders to see the possibilities for change. Called *innovisits*, they are organized, half-day sharing visits between the innovation programs of two or more organizations. During those half-days, the leaders and innovators of one organization visit and learn from the leaders and innovators of another, all in a field-trip show-and-tell method. The visits are very effective at inspiring and igniting new thinking in an organization. By showing one of the organization's leaders how innovation works in another organization (and often another market), leaders can see the art of the possible and better shape their own programs.

Organizations that visit each other can be from the same market or different markets, the same size organization or a different size organization; it's all fair game with innovisits as long as the result includes inspired and energized participants. Sort of like an informal innovation benchmarking for senior leaders, innovisits have proven very beneficial in the Notre Dame iVia innovation program as a method to help senior leaders see practical ways to promote transformation. Phil Newbold, then CEO of Beacon Health, shared his "Innovisit Checklist" for a successful innovisit, attached as an Appendix.

CHAPTER 46

Incubation and Accelerator Memberships

A key strategy used to fend off the symptoms of Victory Disease lies in the utilization of a practice called *incubation*. Incubation and accelerator memberships are innovation collaboration efforts with groups of other organizations that share a market, goal, or challenge. Incubators and accelerators serve to grow or accelerate entrepreneurial endeavors or new solutions. They provide an excellent external resource for innovative ideas and concepts.

An *incubator* is an early-stage place that helps new ideas to grow into more developed ideas. Like an incubator that helps eggs to develop, this place is usually an environment that provides the things that new ideas need to grow and hopefully hatch. Usually the incubation period has no time limit, but ideas do progress through some sort of business case development.

Accelerators, like incubators, help ideas to grow; the difference lies in the set timeline and process of accelerators through which startup companies must progress. The accelerator may have more stringent entrance requirements than an incubator and specific gates that must be achieved. Accelerators, true to their name, accelerate ideas through the development process.

Incubators and accelerators grow new businesses and allow sponsoring participants to realize innovation external to their organization. By sponsoring an incubator or accelerator, an external organization can gain access to a whole host of new business ideas. They also can help them pool resources. Instead of twenty different companies each searching for the same new solution, as well as each spending precious discretionary dollars to pursue them independently, they can consolidate their efforts and spend a fraction of the amount to achieve results. In fact, if the consortium is done right, they can achieve more as part of the group than they could have accomplished alone.

Accelerators tend to have ideas that are more developed than incubators, but both are within the realm of startups (and the terms are frequently interchanged in the non-innovation world). These types of consortiums are gaining popularity within most markets, including my specialty area, financial services. The term *Fintech* is used to describe financial technology startup companies and has become a buzzword due to the proliferation of companies participating in the financial services space.

Examples within financial services include the accelerators that regional banks and credit unions are joining that allow them to compete with the big banks. For example, one of my regional bank clients did not have the resources to pursue digital initiatives at the pace and scale of a large bank such as Citi. Yet they were able to join a digital banking consortium that pooled their resources to develop the same digital solutions as a big bank developed independently. For the consortium, the results are shared among the member organizations for all to benefit.

Another reason that organizations join incubation or accelerator consortiums is to pursue risky or unknown opportunities. The consortium can serve as sort of a hedge against Victory Disease in certain areas. The international consortiums that banks have formed to explore cryptocurrencies offers a prime example. Cryptocurrencies are digital currencies that are alternatives to the dollar. Whereby the current banking system works on centralized control of a standard currency such as the U.S. dollar, cryptocurrencies use a system called *blockchain* to decentralize and digitize exchanges. While the concept is difficult to wrap one's head around, the impact to banks isn't hard to see. If cryptocurrencies took hold, they would immediately disintermediate the entire banking system and plunge banks, both large and small, into bankruptcy. This risk has caused at least 300 U.S. and international banks to form "distributed ledger" groups to research and develop the cryptocurrency technology.

The pros of accelerators and consortiums include the ability to share resources to develop solutions, take on large problems, and share in the results. The downside of these groups lies in their potential to be mismanaged and sometimes even dominated by a few larger donors so smaller donors don't get a say; or they become ruled by a committee-type of management whereby slow, stodgy committees govern the operations, making it cumbersome and bureaucratic. I've sat on some of these incubation committees and witnessed first-hand the inability of the group to move quickly.

Incubators and accelerators both provide another reparative and building device in the toolbox of an organization fighting off Victory Disease. They allow an organization to reach a larger group of entrepreneurial ideas that lie usually outside their organizational structure. However, as with all external endeavors, they must be closely monitored to ensure the strategic objectives are being met without breaking the bank.

CHAPTER 47

Corporate Venture Capital (CVC)

Corporate venture capital (along with mergers and acquisitions) comprises one of the favorite methods of innovation for the senior-most leaders of organizations. Corporate venture capital almost always intrigues my clients who are CEOs or C-suite executives because it involves large money and bold moves. Images of the TV show *Shark Tank* frequently come to their minds.

Corporate venture capital works much like private venture capital, with corporations investing their money into startup type of ventures. Those startups can include very early stage companies literally working out of a garage somewhere, or later stage, more successful, and even profitable companies. The general idea is that the established organization invests in the startup, providing them necessary resources that, in turn, enable the startup to succeed and contribute to the corporation's objectives. The established organization usually ends up with ownership shares of the startup company and, in many cases, gains seats on the startup's Board of Directors.

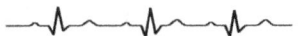

Practical Viewpoint: Interview with Vic Pascucci, Board Member of National Venture Capital Association and a Managing Partner for a Successful VC Firm.

Mick: Do you see Victory Disease in your experiences with corporate America?

Vic: I absolutely see it. Victory Disease is real. The problem is that there is no real incentive for mid-level and senior leaders to disturb the golden goose. If an organization is successful, they don't want to do things that might stop the success of their traditional products and services. The incentives are not to disrupt. Why would they risk a multi-million- or billion-dollar product line if they just want to make it through the next ten years to retire. Even if they see the end coming, it doesn't bother them enough to be motivated to change.

Mick: Is there a solution?

Vic: There is a solution. The solution is a well-organized and aligned organization, with shared values and long-term goals. Organizational alignment and commitment are essential. I'm talking all departments and all leaders focused on a common goal. And those goals must be then aligned and consistent with that of their partners. These are long-term partnerships if we are talking early stage startups. This could be a ten-year-plus commitment. But that is fairly rare.

Mick: You make it sound difficult for a successful organization to overcome Victory Disease. Is it even possible?

Vic: It's possible but not easy. The problem is that most successful organizations are self-centered and only concerned about their own goals. This hurts their ability to truly partner in CVC-type relationships. It prevents them from bringing out the best in their partnerships. Like you, I work a lot in financial services. They are frequently focused on short-term goals and internal politics so that the real innovations aren't possible. The time horizon for partners to disrupt can be ten years. But in ten years a successful corporation can easily have two or three significant leadership changes. Most organizations don't allow for the types of partnerships that are necessary for substantive change. It can be done, but it is rare. Corporations must focus on benefitting their partners more than their own shortsighted needs if they want to create real value and be real partners. They need to appreciate the interests and dynamics of the startups, their co-investors, and the broker ecosystem each operates within.

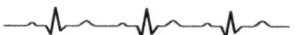

A great recent example of corporate venturing success is illustrated in the investment of American Family Ventures in the Ring video doorbells. Through Ring, the American Family regional insurance carrier was able to enter a new complementary market to their current home insurance space—without having to internally develop expertise in the video doorbell market nor assume the internal risk of a new business.

The primary goal of corporate venture capital focuses on investing in startups that bring strategic value to the organization—which is why it's considered innovation. This differs from private venture capital whose primary goal is usually to earn a return on the investment. While corporate venture capital (CVC) also seeks return on investment, the primary goal should always be to add strategic value to the organization, or in the terms of Victory Disease, it must create antidotes to counter the disease. If done right, CVC can infuse fresh ideas to fill a strategic gap in the sponsoring organization.

The best approaches I've seen have been those companies that have a strong sense of their strategic needs and can apply their efforts to find solutions to fit their gaps. The largest downside to CVC, besides the resources required, is the fact that results are slow acting, requiring three to five years to take hold—and most would consider that quick. Results can take even longer, which means that organizational commitment and understanding are needed at the Board and CEO level. Corporate venture capital, like the mergers and acquisitions method that follows, offers a long-term solution to counter Victory Disease. Notably, organizations can't discard it within the first couple of years; it requires an enduring commitment.

CHAPTER 48

Mergers and Acquisitions

Mergers and acquisitions are the most resource-intensive and laborious of the innovation methods, and also a favorite of senior leaders.

Whereas corporate venture capital lies in the realm of the CEO and C-suite, mergers and acquisitions lie in the realm of their Board members. A merger involves two organizations joining forces, sometimes with a new name, while an acquisition is one company buying another, which is sometimes integrated into the mother company and sometimes run separately as a subsidiary. Mergers and acquisitions are major muscle movements with long-term repercussions that impact the highest levels of the organizations. Not small efforts, they definitely entail two of the key innovation methods for organizations serious about change.

Mergers and acquisitions prove effective against Victory Disease because they enable organizations to gain immediate capabilities and overcome strategic shortcomings in their own. An acquisition is exemplified in the recent purchase of my friend's business TradeKing by Ally Financial. Ally Financial, an online financial services firm, was seeking a digital wealth management capability. TradeKing had established itself as an up-and-coming investment company that used digitization and modern social media tools for investors. Rather than try to build the capability from scratch, Ally Financial invested approximately $275M to purchase TradeKing.[19] For a healthy amount of capital, Ally was able to purchase an innovative and established capability that would have taken a long time and been difficult for them to develop internally. Fast-forward three years to today, and

TradeKing is now Ally Invest, the integrated investment arm for Ally Bank.

One can see another fruitful example of a purchase made to overcome a strategic gap through the Allstate purchase of Esurance. Allstate, one of the largest insurance carriers in the world, has a business model predicated on insurance agents selling policies locally to their clients. The insurance agent has remained one of the cornerstones of Allstate's successful business model. But as the climate changed to a more direct-to-consumer and online experience, Allstate needed a way to reach their customers directly without alienating their existing agents.

Imagine some of the direct-to-market insurance solutions

having to compete with their beloved agents in the field. Innovations would likely not succeed because they would directly threaten their existing model. Thus, enter the acquisition of Esurance, a successful online insurance company dealing directly with consumers. By purchasing Esurance, a separate entity with already successful direct and online solutions, Allstate was able to change and adapt without alienating their very strong agent base. They essentially created a buffer between their new business model and existing model, minimizing the conflict. The greater Allstate organization now touts a viable direct-to-consumer model as well as their tried-and-true agents in the field. Allstate avoided directly cannibalizing themselves while still taking advantage of the emerging online and direct market that Esurance provided.

Alexander the Great, our historical innovation leader, also successfully used mergers to expand his empire. When Alexander conquered a region or city, he sought to colonize as much as possible. In a political sense, he pursued the merger and acquisition approach for growth. In one example, after Alexander conquered Northern India, he allowed the king of the area to remain in power because Alexander was impressed with his courage and leadership. In another example of mergers, Alexander moved to unite the Persians with his Macedonian rulers. Alexander rightly saw this strategy as a way to rapidly transform his empire. To accomplish this goal, he ordered eighty of his Macedonian companions to marry Persian princesses—merger by marriage. Alexander himself led by example and married a high-ranking Persian daughter to solidify his rule. The ultimate result was that the Persians joined Alexander's Macedonian forces as loyal soldiers of Alexander. While arranged marriages will likely not occur in our modern organizations, shared goals of leaders are used to fuel successful mergers and acquisitions.

Since mergers and acquisitions comprise such major moves, they are also the riskiest. Large expenses are involved, and organizational cultures are changed forever. But as an innovation method, mergers and acquisitions remain two of the most aggressive methods to use for countering Victory Disease. They are the equivalent of an organ transplant to keep a person alive and, in some cases, can be a bionic implant that makes the organism superior. Regardless, they are key methods to fight Victory Disease and sometimes the best way for an organization to maintain long-term viability.

The Innovation Journey

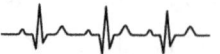

"There's a way to do it better – find it."

Thomas A. Edison

CHAPTER 49

The Customer Is Medic, Nurse, and Doctor

The quintessential consideration for innovation is the customer. The customer sits alone as the most important aspect of innovation, and anyone that tells you differently isn't paying attention. The customer is why we innovate and whom we innovate for. Because of that, customers must be included in every step and every process—just as if they own the process—because they ARE the owner. They are the medics that provide immediate response. The nurses that conduct the daily and long-term care. And the doctors that oversee the entire disease response.

The customer expects to get what they want, how they want it, when they want it. The days of a handful of organizational leaders sitting in a building and unilaterally deciding what products to offer customers are gone. The customer is the essential element of everything innovation—they are the raison d'être, the reason for being innovative. When that central truth is realized and operationalized, new ideas succeed; and when organizations ignore the importance of the customer, they fail.

It's too easy for successful organizations to ignore the growing influence of the customer as they overconfidently proceed on their formerly fruitful paths. I see it all the time in financial services. The arrogant actions of Bank of America (discussed earlier) in which they unilaterally levied an additional charge to debit card users was a gross undercalculation of the power of the customer. They did so without considering the feelings or responses of their customers because they ignored the growing clout of the end-user. Those customers revolted and forced a hasty retreat of a major bank, causing serious brand damage. In the age of social media, customers project a strong voice.

In my experience, the very best innovations entail those that take care of the customer's needs first, not as an afterthought. When I led the innovation program at a large financial services firm that was ranked first in customer service, we earnestly put the customer in the center of our innovation process (although it wasn't easy). I witnessed how serving the customer first ensured new solutions that truly met customer needs and weren't in conflict with the organization's revenue objectives.

Perhaps the situation is clarified by picturing two competing gods that want to be served: a revenue-growth god and a customer-experience god. The revenue-growth god is usually more powerful and demanding within the organizational culture. Revenue is omnipresent and all powerful. People are promoted or fired based on it, bonuses are tied to it, and talk about it dominates. It demands daily sacrifices and front-page attention. Meanwhile, the customer-benefit god sits on the sidelines as an unassuming and modest god, entering the picture only when the organization invites its viewpoint into the decision cycles.

But here's the catch. Although quiet and unassuming, the customer-service god is really the more powerful and independent of the two. It recognizes true customer services innovations and naturally grows them. When a company or innovation doesn't support the customer-benefit god and, instead, only pursues revenue goals, its customers are able to quickly notice the lack of benefit for them and migrate elsewhere. However, when the customer-service god is served, then customers magically gravitate towards the new innovations. And in our modern environment, a multiplicity effect is created by the customer's pleasure or displeasure. Each customer has enormous power to support or dislike ideas. If customers promote an idea, they can become informal brand ambassadors who ultimately create more demand for the new idea (which generates revenue). Because the customer-service god is greater, whenever a successful idea serves the customer god, the revenue god will always follow it. Customer service and customer experience should always lead innovations when a choice exists.

CHAPTER 50

Stop Committing Seppuku and Enjoy the Journey

There is a popular Zen story I like to use to show the predicament of groups succumbing to Victory Disease. The story is about a *Zen master, tiger, strawberry*, and *cliff*. In the story I like to think of the *strawberry* as both innovation and its pursuit. The message of the story illustrates the difficult situation in which leaders find themselves in the advanced stages of Victory Disease. While many versions of the story exist, mine goes like this:

> There was a Zen master out walking one spring day when he suddenly came upon a tiger. The tiger chased the master towards the top of a high cliff, which was too steep to climb down. But a small branch was sticking out from the cliff's edge. The master had no choice but to hang onto the branch and dangle over the side. The hungry tiger was above him and death was below him. He looked at the branch and saw a ripe, red strawberry on the branch. He reached up, grabbed the strawberry, and ate it. The master was heard to say, "This lovely strawberry, how sweet it tastes."

This story illustrates the approach you must take if you find you're in an organization in the late stages of Victory Disease. It entails a perilous situation not unlike many organizations are in today, one very difficult to overcome. Einstein's famous comment that "we cannot solve our problems with the same thinking we used when we created them" applies to this dilemma. The organization hangs precariously, in a very bad situation. The tiger will eat you above and the drop will kill you below. The *tiger* represents the past poor decisions, and the *cliff* is the future impending death. You cannot wholly focus on either, but in these perilous circumstances you must find a way to embrace innovation (i.e., the strawberry) to escape. Only in a resolved embracing of the new, fun, and spontaneous lies the potential to overcome the disease.

A pop culture example of overcoming the disease through fun and spontaneity is the story of Sammy Hagar. Sammy Hagar, some might recall, was a famous rock-'n-roller who rose to prominence in the '70s and '80s. He was a soloist and guitarist who achieved fame performing first as himself, the "Red Rocker." He achieved several hit records that made him a superstar. In 1985, after a successful solo career, he went on to become the lead singer for a popular '80s band called Van Halen. The Van Halen band, sometimes dubbed "Van Hagar" for the time Hagar was part of it, produced an abundance of hit songs and albums, selling out venues for the next four years. But at the height of their success, the band leader, Eddie Van Halen, unceremoniously released Hagar. To put it bluntly, Sammy Hagar was fired. To make it worse, he was fired under a cloud of unfavorable comparisons between Hagar and the former lead vocalist. Hagar now found himself in a bad position— an aging lead singer without a band and with bad press. The Sammy Hagar brand tumbled into a death spiral and had every reason to continue falling.

But the Hagar story didn't end there, precisely because of his ability to find the strawberry hanging off the branch. Just like the Zen master facing perils on both sides, so Sammy Hagar also was seemingly at the end of his run. He had been fired from one of the most popular rock bands of the time, he was facing unfavorable comparisons with their old lead singer, and he was aging. Some musicians have been known to retire in seclusion or begin overusing drugs at such critical downturns in their lives. But, even in these difficult circumstances, Sammy Hagar was able to embrace the fun of his existence. Like the Zen master, Hagar appreciated the moment and found a way to overcome his malaise instead of dwelling on the tiger above or the cliff below.

Hagar's "strawberry" manifested itself when he decided to create his own brand of tequila as well as invest his time in his resort in Cabo San Lucas, Mexico. He transformed his brand by having fun. He performed in Cabo for his friends, made spirits, and enjoyed life. He didn't pay attention to the rock pundits saying he was washed up or at the very real end of his massive music following. He enjoyed the moment, and through that enjoyment found a new avenue for the Sammy Hagar brand to prosper.

The Hagar brand became all about fun and good spirits. The Cabo Wabo resort gained a cult following, the spirits became popular and profitable (the tequila brand was sold for $91M[20]), and Hagar became synonymous with enjoying life. Fast forward to the writing of this book, and we find the Sammy Hagar brand completely reinvented. It's not pretentious or arrogant, but a fun-loving brand. Notwithstanding, the brand now encompasses multiple good liquors, restaurants, a club that is constantly sold out, a new band, and a popular TV show hosted by Hagar himself. His brand was at near death, but by tasting the strawberry he was able to let the fun outcome of new adventures recreate his brand. Hagar says the Cabo Wabo resort ". . . was not business. It was strictly passion. It has turned into an unbelievable business." Using his previous capital, he reinvented his brand through tequila, restaurants, and bars. He demonstrates that when Victory Disease appears terminal, the newness of change and innovation must be embraced.

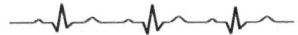

Practical Viewpoint: How I Brought Ashley Stewart Back from Bankruptcy—by James Rhee[1]

In 2013, Ashley Stewart, the plus-size fashion company, was on the brink of bankruptcy — its second in a little over three years. Decades of operating losses and rampant turnover in both the employee base and ownership group had cemented a fearful culture. The fast-turning nature of the company's inventory and the constant specter of insolvency undermined long-term investments and strategic planning. The company did not even have Wi-Fi at its corporate headquarters—a dark, converted warehouse that time had forgotten. The nascent e-commerce effort, viewed suspiciously by most in the company, operated independently on an antiquated platform.

I did not want the company to liquidate. I had been a member of the board since 2011 and loved the brand and everything it stood for. Ashley Stewart had been founded to provide plus-size fashion for women in boutique-like settings in urban neighborhoods across the United States. After listening to our customers, I came to realize that the brand stood for more than that — values like respect, empowerment, and joy. In tightly knit communities, shopping routines are interwoven amongst generations of women, often around important moments for them like church, family reunions, or a new job interview. In short, I felt Ashley Stewart stood for kindness and embodied community.

To give her a chance, I resigned from the board to become CEO in August 2013. I decided I'd give it six months and my best shot. On my first day, I confessed to the entire home office and field management team that I was the least qualified person to run the business. After all, as a long-tenured private equity investor and former high school teacher, I had never been an employee of a fashion brand or retailer, let alone held the CEO title. I imagine that this was of small comfort to a fractured company less than three years removed from one bankruptcy and six months away from a second. Things probably only got worse when I concluded my first town hall meeting with a statement that kindness, as the bedrock of innovation and consumer engagement, was a go-forward core strategic pillar.

For the next six months, leading up to our March 2014 bankruptcy filing, we relied on math, changing the company culture, a mission-driven dedication to our core customer, transparent communication, lean processes and—yes—kindness:

Changing the company culture: We knocked down walls to create a more open floor plan, and I immediately shut down the C-suite offices and moved into a cubicle. In July 2014, following our emergence from bankruptcy in April 2014, we moved to a new office, on a shoe-string— basically moving ourselves in U-Hauls. I still do not have an office. I sit at a desk, with no drawers, in the middle of a wide open, trading floor-type space. There is no correlation between seniority and office size—only those who need real quiet to do their jobs get offices. We've also gotten rid of most formal job descriptions. Most of the management team could not adapt to the new professional services-type environment, while others were doomed by our new startup mentality. Those who could adapt, thrived. In the end, we downsized corporate headcount by 40 percent.

Operations streamlined around the core customer: With our core customer's needs foremost in mind, we closed almost 100 stores, renegotiated or rejected close to 150 executory contracts, re-platformed the website, outsourced all distribution, and virtualized our fleet of servers. We also made sure the algorithms we were using for goods flow and markdown cadence had been derived from close study of, first, our customers' psyche and emotional tendencies, and, second, their physical shopping behaviors. We did all of this in six months with a skeleton team.

Transparent communication. We outlined in advance every step, and we took great care to explain why our decisions were best for Ashley Stewart and her customers. We used SMS, email, and social media to engage directly with our customer, and we had very direct conversations with our field associates. By broadcasting our operational changes this way, we helped engender trust and build a foundation for the open-door policy of our new social-first, mobile-delivered customer engagement strategy.

Kindness: Despite our financial plight, we reintroduced a generous local charitable giving program during the 2013 holiday season. We were penniless, frightened, and exhausted, but we knew that our philanthropic efforts were the right thing to do on multiple levels. A picture from our YWCA event in Brooklyn still hangs next to my desk to this day. It reminds me daily of the importance of staying true to core values, a commitment I made to my father, who dedicated his life to the well-being of children.

Today, Ashley Stewart is thriving. Operating profits are at unprecedented levels, organic sales growth is north of 25 percent, and our asset productivity, through the implementation of lean processes, has shot up. Our digital business is booming. Our e-commerce business accounts for roughly one-third of total net sales, and it is growing at over an 80 percent clip. Our mobile metrics are particularly encouraging, with demand growth at 200-plus percent and demand penetration at well north of 30 percent of total e-commerce demand. We're also seeing some of the highest levels of social media engagement amongst all brands. We are one of the largest, most profitable, and fastest growing plus-size fashion brands in the world.

My six-month stint is now turning into a two-year anniversary. Looking back, I realize that in some ways, we were blessed with how broken the business model was and how dire the circumstances were. We got the opportunity to rewrite everything from scratch. The bankruptcy process allowed us to re-assess and renegotiate all vendor relationships. We were also lucky, and good—our small team, without the help of a single third-party consultant, executed seamlessly on a well-scripted set of operational changes, any one of which could have ended the company had it gone wrong.

But I still believe that the single biggest contributor to our success has been the fostering of a teaching culture with deep roots in kindness. Kindness enables innovation by creating a safe work environment, and it serves as the foundation for our meritocratic, performance-based culture. Kindness also supports our fiduciary-type sensibility towards our customer.

We are a mission-driven business—we believe in advocating for a woman who could sometimes use more advocacy. Everything we do is to serve her.

Period. And she has led the way forward for us. She has driven us to become a global leader in social media. She is driving us to explore enhancements to our nascent mobile capabilities. And yet until and unless she cares, we are not concerned in the least about winning a "Store of the Future" award. Indeed, some of our most innovative forms of consumer engagement are laughably old-fashioned, like "sip and shop" events and in-store model searches. We are investing heavily in customer service and employee training, because we believe that's what she wants. And we will continue to work hard for her and show her the respect she deserves.

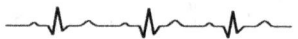

Chapter 51
Have Fun

Innovation must be fun. This concept is simple, but so hard for serious-minded organizations to wrap their heads around. They are so caught up in the rigor and discipline of success that they forget to enjoy what they're doing. But *fun* must be incorporated into every innovation effort. In the innovation world, there is no such thing as miserable team members or miserable customers. Our teammates and our customers want to have fun. And no one wants to be miserable. Yes, launching new ideas and new organizations can be hard work, but the entrepreneurial organization finds ways to motivate their people to enjoy working hard.

A Volkswagen initiative termed "The Fun Theory" illustrates that people's behavior can be influenced for the better by making their efforts fun. In a test in Sweden, Volkswagen set up musical piano steps on the staircase of a subway station. When you climbed each step, it made a piano note sound. Why? Their goal was to see if people would choose the more cumbersome stairs over the escalator if they made the stairs more fun to climb. Remarkably, they found that 66 percent more people took the stairs than had previously taken them when the stairs weren't fun. It was the same stairs as before, same height, same effort required to climb; but people were way more inclined to take on the stair climb when it was perceived as fun and different. The conclusion of the experiment is one that innovators already knew: that fun can be a compelling motivation. This is always the case for new ideas and initiatives. Fun will make the work seem easier and more fulfilling.

If you look at innovation centers or entrepreneurial offices where people introduce change, they are noticeably more interesting than the regular business places. They look different—many have the collaborative and open workstations, others have the obligatory hanging suspended palm trees, and yet others have different-colored walls and floors to remind participants that their work should be fun. The corporate standards are usually dismissed in favor of fun and outrageous things, sometimes even childlike. They recognize the fun factor in innovation and hope to bring it through the environment. And while no one has ever said that successful change is easy, fun must be a part of the effort or it will likely fail. Fun is an essential component of the Victory Disease antidote.

Chapter 52

Full Circle: The U.S. Military and Victory Disease

Far too many market leaders are infected with the dreaded Victory Disease and are doomed to fail unless they change. The battle for market dominance will go to the agile and innovative. Successful, modern businesses are repeating the history of the Japanese collapse by ignoring the ABCs of Victory Disease.

This book has taken a fairly obscure military concept and applied it to the malaise present in most of the successful organizations in the world. So, in the concluding chapter, it proves fitting to apply the concept when looking at the strongest fighting and defending force in the world: the United States military. Are the elements of Victory Disease present even there?

I spent small portions of the book providing my personal stories of digitization in the military and bragging about the amazing innovations that gave the U.S. military superior technological advantages, ones that brought tacticians' dreams to life. To know accurately the location of your troops on the ground, to know both their statuses and those of your enemies, and to use that information to maneuver in ways the enemy deemed impossible—it was miraculous. The U.S. military has been riding waves of technological superiority and seems poised to continue. But are they?

Certainly, the military and political leaders convey the continuance of victory and dominance. A real confidence in U.S. military power rests on far-reaching assumptions of continuing technological and information superiority. American military commanders are now used to leveraging the best equipment and information to achieve victory. The U.S. is building more and more capabilities based on those assumptions, with the current military leaders constantly talking about making the military "bigger and stronger." But I see all that confidence translating into more group incremental thinking.

The situation is akin to the Japanese building the biggest battleships ever constructed as their solution to continued success. They didn't recognize new methods for warfighting, such as air power, and assumed the conditions of war would stay constant. Likewise, the U.S. is assuming away the new nonlinear and asymmetric battlefields of terrorism. Because the U.S. has won so many victories on the conventional battlefield, they want to perpetuate the same conditions. But those same conditions don't exist. Terrorism has forever changed the people, places, and methods of warfare. Yet the U.S. stays in denial, even to the point of calling it a *war on terror*, and deploying conventional troops to try to combat unconventional threats. It's not working and looks like it will never really work. Much like the Japanese avoided the inevitable role of airpower in World War II, the U.S. seems fixated on ignoring the nonconventional aspects of modern warfare, continuing to expend most of their energy and resources on the incremental improvements of warfare.

As a veteran of the Afghanistan War and publisher of a book on our Army-building role there, I can look back with honesty now after 17 years and clearly see we have been victims of all three symptoms in the Afghanistan region—specifically, in the nation-building effort in Afghanistan that started with the onset of that war in 2001. By the time the combat operations were declared over in 2014, the Afghanistan War had become the longest war ever fought by the United States. And just declaring it over doesn't make it so, as we can still see military operations (and casualties) to this date. So how did Victory Disease creep into the U.S. operations in Afghanistan?

First and foremost, Americans were arrogant. We assumed that by merely pumping money and troops into Afghanistan we could change centuries-long cultural issues and norms. An Afghanistan saying declares, "The King only rules in Kabul," which symbolizes the independence of the various provinces and tribes. Yet, the United States tended to ignore the significant role of the various parts of Afghanistan and how disparate they are. When Americans think of a country, we tend to think of a unified body of people with the same language and beliefs. We forced our definition of a country on them, much like Britain did in the 1800s. However, Afghanistan is just the opposite and is unified on Western maps only by a physical outline; in reality, it encompasses a diverse collection of ethnicities, tribes, languages, and social beliefs. When asked for identification, a person in the countryside would respond with the name of his tribe or ethnic group. He would not respond that he was an Afghan because most Afghanis don't think of themselves as Afghanistan citizens. Their self-identification with their tribes would be akin to someone asking me what country I was from, and me responding that I was "of the Providence Simonelli clan of the New England Region." Only in the capital city of Kabul resided some Afghanistan citizens who identified with the country. The rest of Afghanistan is pure tribal identification.

Since Afghanistan was the crossroads to the East, most of the major powers of the past two centuries had left some kind of mark on the people. The various invaders left permanent impressions in the rugged terrain of Afghanistan, making it a country of tribes. Small, mud-brick guardhouses litter the countryside. The guard shacks are strategically placed to overlook key terrain or large plains. Once manned by British sentries, they are occupied by whatever tribe happens to control the region. Over seventy different tribes are recognized in Afghanistan, each with its own hierarchical systems and customs, and each speaking a different dialect or language. We, for the most part, arrogantly ignored those key realities, assuming that our definition of "country" would influence them just because of our money and military.

The bureaucracy and complacency of our operation there is stifling. We have committed enough resources to build multiple nations from scratch, yet Afghanistan did not develop the way we planned. The United States has committed somewhere around six trillion dollars,[21] way less than the estimates to cure world hunger. As of this writing, there have also been about 3,500 deaths and 20,000 injured in and around Afghanistan.[22] Yet we still have very little to show for our efforts. I personally was involved in spending large amounts of our initial investment and am disappointed that our labors were so wasteful. Yet we complacently continue to pump military and dollars into the region.

But the Afghanistan War isn't the only event subject to Victory Disease. The most effective military in the world is experiencing Victory Disease because it assumes its opponents will operate on American terms, even as it sees example after example of war being waged in nonconventional ways. The plan to remain dominant by seeing a common operating picture on a digital battlefield from the comfort of a war-room, where everything is seen and known to U.S. commanders, illustrates complete arrogance. If terrorism continues on its path, one can easily envision war continuing to grow in nontraditional, more guerilla-style battlespaces like cities or civilian dwellings. If so, the U.S. military will be surprised and caught without their conventional advantages.

Even though the concept of Victory Disease originated within the military, the U.S. is running blindly to support suggestions of continued dominance, with little recognition of that disease. As of the writing of this book, the proposed 2021 U.S. defense budget request is a whopping $705B dollars[23]—spending more money on defense than most countries' entire gross domestic product, with the one revolutionary initiative being the establishment of the Space Force. Yet, the vast majority of America's warpower is tied up in legacy programs and conventional warfare products. One can't help but see the resemblance to the World War II Japanese. Meanwhile, the United States has become the world's largest debtor, setting the stage for a major meltdown when things go wrong.

The U.S. military is spending massively on its legacy programs, even in the face of significant evidence of a changing, unconventional battlefield. Much like the WWII Japanese, so too the United States military pursues a continuance of past warfighting successes while avoiding the hard decisions about the future.

Conclusion

The impact of Victory Disease extends everywhere but is more visible in certain industries and organizations. Everything is changing, with innovation rapidly accelerating. Virtually anything that can be automated will be. Anything that can be commoditized and reduced to online competition will be. Customer involvement and ownership of products and services will continue to grow. The digitization of the world is happening now. Disruption has become the new normal as most successful organizations still struggle with its reality.

The vigilant organizations will emerge the successful ones, those who see their own ABCs of Victory Disease and take prudent actions to defeat them. Some industries and areas are more prone to contract Victory Disease than others. Numerous markets such as media, retail, and traditional education are susceptible. The genetics of these industries just makes them more likely to acquire one or more symptoms. As the world rapidly transforms, they sit in denial, struggling to find successful strategies to overcome the disease.

But we also need to look to the thriving industries to see where Victory Disease is most prevalent. Many successful organizations have become victims of previously proven business models and have promoted their leaders based on adherence to these status quo models. Many have allowed malignant elements to become embedded in their culture, which prevents them from making changes necessary at the pace required. For many organizations, Victory Disease looms as a near-term threat.

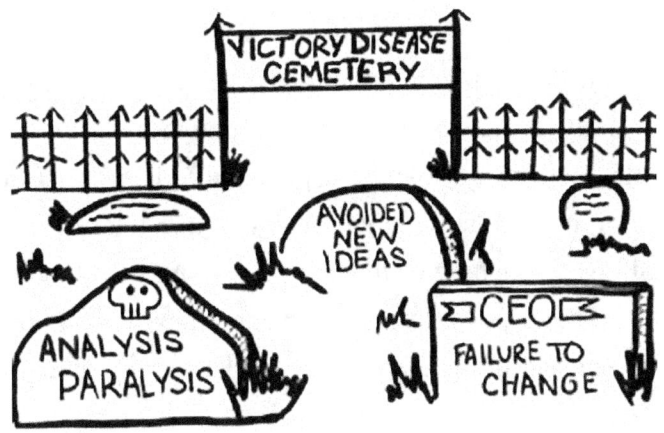

My market of financial services is under threat and slowly starting to realize it. Yet, most of the market shareholders aren't doing much to counter the threats. One merely needs to look at the incrementalism of large banks, insurance, and investment companies. They possess all three of the symptoms—as arrogant, highly bureaucratic, and complacent organizations.

We can see that all industries and all organizations are prone to Victory Disease in this hyper-innovation environment. Just as individuals who look out for their health have a greater likelihood to enjoy healthy days, so organizations that are aware of and work to counter their vulnerabilities are more likely to find disease-conquering ways. The ABCs are real—they gain footholds in healthy organizations and infect the organizational culture. If not recognized and treated, they spread. The symptoms must be confronted head-on. Like with cancer, they must undergo routine testing to detect its signs, and when found, rapidly eliminated.

Arrogance is perhaps the easiest to detect, characterized by an organization that has stopped seeking, listening, and learning. These leaders know what is right without feedback, usually valuing their own internal opinions over anything else. They exhibit rigidity in decision-making, avoiding ideas that don't agree with their own. An arrogant organization is not particularly receptive to market or customer feedback. In Victory Disease, an organizational hardening of the arteries sets in, with the free flow of ideas and concepts becoming more and more constrained until the artery eventually closes to new ideas . . . and then the organization dies.

Bureaucracy, the slow and steady symptom of Victory Disease, resides everywhere that organizations are growing. Bureaucracy entails a necessary evil for maturing organizations because it encourages standardization and policies. Imagine trying to navigate a payment system in a global organization without some polices in place—a nightmare would ensue. But processes can become overly rigid, formal, and self-serving. The same helpful bureaucracy that improves the organization slowly grows into a deliberate, impersonal killer of anything new or transformational. Bureaucracy kills new initiatives through process and formality. I have witnessed more innovations die through a bureaucratic project approval process than any other way. Wonderful, amazing ideas enter the bureaucracy, only to be neutralized or scaled down to a fragment of the original idea. The bureaucracy becomes a muscle that can perform only one rigid exercise, and when another type of muscle move is needed, the bureaucracy can't adjust. Bureaucracy kills.

Complacency is the third and perhaps hardest of the Victory Disease symptoms to notice, as what the organization is NOT doing brings it to light. Equally comfortable in small or large organizations, complacency stems from a feeling of success and accomplishment long after such a feeling is warranted. Complacent organizations don't look for new opportunities or hazards and are, instead, happy with the status quo. The (now forgotten) Digital Equipment Corporation is one of the poster children for complacency when, at the top of the computer industry in the 1990s, they decided to continue with their strategy in the face of microcomputers' emergence. Their CEO's statement summed up complacency nicely when he asserted, "There is no reason for any individual to have a computer in his home."[24] Of course, when the CEO of a major organization complacently avoids recognizing real threats, the rest of the leadership is likely to follow. As with the Digital Equipment Corporation, complacency in Victory Disease rapidly spreads to groupthink that involves most of the organization. In complacent organizations, the status quo reigns supreme.

Victory Disease defines a dire sickness, a nasty organizational malady. But many ways exist to overcome Victory Disease. I have outlined some of the methods and tactics that prove useful. But before committing resources to an innovation program, the first step entails a healthy and honest examination of the organization. Examine what it has done well and what it hasn't. How are new ideas developed, and how are the people who bring them forward treated? Listen to the customers and what they are telling you. And lastly, watch the market. What is happening in your market?

The World War II Japanese held to their formerly successful ways until the bitter end, many times preferring to commit seppuku rather than seek alternatives or admit failure. It didn't need to be so, as their military analysts later diagnosed. They did, however, have a blaring requirement to acknowledge their arrogance, bureaucracy, and complacency. Unfortunately, they weren't capable of recognizing their own Victory Disease until too late.

I modified the Japanese Victory Disease assessment to look at existing successful organizations and found that, in comparison, we are even more inclined to fall victim to the dreaded disease. Although I used the Japanese example as a frame for this book, I am in no way implying that they were the only organization susceptible to the disease—just the first to be recognized for its existence and symptoms. As a result, the Japanese military in World War II suffered one of the worst defeats in modern history after one of the most successful starts. Arrogance, bureaucracy, and complacency were catalysts for infecting their successful efforts, and like so many others, causing their demise. Now in our hyper-innovation environment, that same fate will fall upon many organizations today—but more rapidly. Will organizations recognize their symptoms and treat the underlying causes before it's too late?

Appendix A
Innovisit Checklist

Practical Case: Beacon Health's 21 Points for a Successful Innovisit

1.   Why It's Important – Site visits are the most efficient, quickest, and most effective way to increase the learning curve about Innovation. You are learning from those who have been there, often with decades of experience, insights, and learning. It is a very effective way to use scarce time and resources for busy leaders, Board members, and physicians. Finally, site visits are extremely energizing and rapidly build support for the new way with key leaders.

2.   Common Barriers – Big egos from senior management are the biggest barriers to even considering personally going on an exploration site visit. Having the courage to admit that you don't know much about Innovation and then going personally (as opposed to delegating someone) is the necessary first step in changing your culture to one that supports creativity and new ideas. The second barrier is the fear of looking stupid or expressing naivety about a new field of management. Going out on an exploration to an unknown territory of the business world can appear scary, but nearly everyone started his or her journey in this same way. Finally, a lack of knowledge on how to set up the site visit, how to conduct an effective session, and how to capture the learnings can appear as large drawbacks. These 21 points will provide enough to get started, and combined with your enthusiasm for the adventure, you will have all that's needed.

3.   Why the Host Company Welcomes You – First, your visit

will be welcomed by the senior leadership, especially if you are an existing or potential customer for them. Aren't you proud to give tours of your organization and answer questions about how you got to be so successful? Put aside your competitive feelings, and the host will be flattered that you think they are innovative, that they are being benchmarked against, and that they can help change another organization (that really needs it). Besides, the visit might lead to some new business and strengthen their existing and future relationships.

4.   Developing the Prospect List – Start with your existing large suppliers and vendors who are recognized leaders with a regular flow of new products and services and an established track record in innovation. Local companies that have R&D budgets also help you identify new terms and tactics; plus, visits are easier to schedule with less travel time. You will probably need to sit down with your purchasing department and get an idea of your purchasing volumes with major suppliers, which will be necessary information to know for the site visit.

5.   Stay Away from Sales – Probably the hardest job will be to identify the right person who can steer you to the R&D or product development leaders. Aim too high and you won't find a sympathetic ear or will have problems with tight schedules. Aim too low and you may not be talking to people who know the innovation process and the history of its evolution. Above all, stay away from pure sales staff, as you will only be viewed as a potential customer and you will only receive a very long, elaborate sales presentation.

6.   Doing Your Homework – Research your site visit company very thoroughly. Know how much you are buying from them or one of their competitors. Carefully review their website, last 2-3

annual reports, top executives, and news articles. Do a good web search. Take along or send in advance a brief description of your organization and its top leadership.

7.   Making Your Initial Contact – Always assign a senior leader to make your initial contact, and be very clear of whom you want to meet with by title or function (the head of R&D, the person responsible for new product development). Never delegate this responsibility to an assistant, and you might have to use others to make an introduction or to make an initial contact. Always ask at the host company who they think is doing great innovative work and if they could open some doors or make some contacts for you. Network, network, network!!

8.   Explaining Your Purpose – Outline why you are interested in Innovation and why their company was chosen. Be firm that you are just learning and want to bring a small team of senior leaders. Ask for about two hours with their leadership, but almost all visits run much longer as the passion and enthusiasm begin to flow.

9.   Who Goes on the Visit – The small group of leaders who are very passionate and enthusiastic should lead the small team. Always take along an enthusiastic Board member and maybe someone new each time from senior management. An ideal size is five to six persons, but any size if it's not too large can capture the learning and build future relationships. Think of these visits as repeatable and always be on the lookout for speakers and presenters for your management education days and Board retreats.

10. Make a List of Questions – Always draw up an extensive list of questions beforehand and share with everyone. At first the questions will be very general, but after a few site visits, you will be able to ask better questions and have knowledge from which to

compare and contrast. Ask further clarifying questions on any terms or concept you don't understand. Remember, you are a sponge and need to understand what the presenter is saying.

11. Sample Questions – Start out by asking who is responsible for new product/service development, what background/training they have, where they go for professional development and meetings, and what literature they read and/or publish in. Ask what process they use for generating new ideas, where the process came from, who is directly involved in new idea formation, and how deep in the organization they go to find new ideas. What are the budget thresholds for new ideas, prototypes, or new businesses, and who should approve what at what level? Finally, ask what the major obstacles, barriers, and roadblocks are that keep them awake at night, that get in the way of the innovation process. Also ask, if they had it to do over again, what might they do differently, and what are the lessons learned by any failures and unsuccessful ventures?

12. Your Objectives – Almost every site visit began with a request by the host for us to clearly set out our hospital's objectives in the journey of Innovation. What did we want innovation to do for our customers and for our organization? Be clear as to what your initial objectives are, and be prepared to adapt and modify them as your knowledge increases.

13. Non-disclosures – Some organizations may want you to sign a non-disclosure form before they will start the meeting. This protects their intellectual property rights and is a very wise thing to do for all parties. The host takes the protection of this intangible asset very seriously, and you should also. You probably will not be able to modify the agreement at all, but you can limit its duration to a year or two.

14. Sponges, Learning, Listening – One of the reasons for having a small group of learners is that often each person has a different perspective on what they heard or team members miss what is being presented because they are taking notes or in a side conversation. Try to clarify all aspects of what is presented and always ask what other options or choices were considered every step of the way. Ask if you can get some answers to follow-up questions after you have a few days to digest what you learned and everyone has had a chance to debrief. This helps with a second visit or important follow-up opportunities and partnerships.

15. Returning the Favor – At first, the site visits will be one-way learning, but after a few experiences you may be able to help your host with some new information, new articles, or a website that you came upon. This makes the visit a real win-win for all parties and helps develop your personal network.

16. Opportunities to Partner – Always keep your antenna up for future opportunities to testbed new products and services, serve as a beta site for a new prototype, or jointly develop a new product. Many organizations are looking for innovative companies to gain access to key capabilities to evaluate future needs. Being able to spot a good opportunity is a very valuable skill, and possibilities should be evaluated at the end of every site visit.

17. Write Up Learnings Immediately – On the way home or very shortly thereafter, commit yourself to a formal debriefing with as many as possible. Write down all your observations, lessons learned, steps in the Innovation process, key people you met and their phone numbers and e-mail, and points for further clarification. Circulate your learnings to your senior leadership and enthusiastically review the key points with all those who are interested.

18. Follow-up with a Thank You – Always follow-up immediately with a personal thank you note (never e-mail) to those who shared their experiences. Be sure to let them know how much you learned and how valuable the site visit was to your future planning. Let them know if there are any other follow-up items due from you, and be sure to honor your commitments.

19. Small Gifts – Either when you finish the site visit or as a "thank you" soon after, it is great to give each presenter a small gift from your organization. The more innovative and clever the better, so someone should be assigned to come up with just the right gift. Real home-run visits should include a great gift basket to express your thanks for sharing so much of their learning.

20. Identifying Contact Persons – Always assign one person to be your organizational chief contact person for follow-up and to really work on the ongoing relationship. Remember to keep your host involved in all your successes (and good failures) and to return any favors from your organization. Watch the business news to follow your host's new products and their business successes.

21. Help with Leads and Introductions – Always keep in mind opportunities to supply your host company with important leads for new business. Often you will know about a new building project or a new physician group to whom you can make an introduction and help establish a good contact. As your partnerships and networks grow, you will become an important organization to many, all because you first started out as a naïve, newcomer to the field of innovation who just picked up the phone and began the exploration.

Appendix B
Amazon CEO Letter

Following is a 2016 Amazon CEO letter to shareholders that succinctly captures some of the challenges with avoiding Victory Disease.

"Jeff, what does Day 2 look like?"

That's a question I just got at our most recent all-hands meeting. I've been reminding people that it's Day 1 for a couple of decades. I work in an Amazon building named Day 1, and when I moved buildings, I took the name with me. I spend time thinking about this topic.

"Day 2 is stasis. Followed by irrelevance. Followed by excruciating, painful decline. Followed by death. And that is why it's always Day 1."

To be sure, this kind of decline would happen in extreme slow motion. An established company might harvest Day 2 for decades, but the final result still comes.

I'm interested in the question, how do you fend off Day 2? What are the techniques and tactics? How do you keep the vitality of Day 1, even inside a large organization?

Such a question can't have a simple answer. There will be many elements, multiple paths, and many traps. I don't know the whole answer, but I may know bits of it. Here's a starter pack of essentials for Day 1 defense: customer obsession, a skeptical view of proxies, the eager adoption of external trends, and high-velocity decision-making.

True Customer Obsession

There are many ways to center a business. You can be

competitor focused, you can be product focused, you can be technology focused, you can be business model focused, and there are more. But in my view, obsessive customer focus is by far the most protective of Day 1 vitality.

Why? There are many advantages to a customer-centric approach, but here's the big one: customers are always beautifully, wonderfully dissatisfied, even when they report being happy and business is great. Even when they don't yet know it, customers want something better, and your desire to delight customers will drive you to invent on their behalf. No customer ever asked Amazon to create the Prime membership program, but it sure turns out they wanted it, and I could give you many such examples.

Staying in Day 1 requires you to experiment patiently, accept failures, plant seeds, protect saplings, and double down when you see customer delight. A customer-obsessed culture best creates the conditions where all of that can happen.

Resist Proxies

As companies get larger and more complex, there's a tendency to manage to proxies. This comes in many shapes and sizes, and it's dangerous, subtle, and very Day 2.

A common example is process as proxy. Good process serves you so you can serve customers. But if you're not watchful, the process can become the thing.

This can happen very easily in large organizations. The process becomes the proxy for the result you want. You stop looking at outcomes and just make sure you're doing the process right. Gulp. It's not that rare to hear a junior leader defend a bad outcome with something like, "Well, we followed the process." A more experienced leader will use it as an opportunity to investigate and improve the process. The process is not the thing. It's always worth asking, do we own the process or does the process own us? In a Day 2 company, you might find it's the second.

Another example: market research and customer surveys can become proxies for customers—something that's especially dangerous when you're inventing and designing products. "Fifty-five percent of beta testers report being satisfied with this feature. That is up from 47% in the first survey." That's hard to interpret and could unintentionally mislead.

Good inventors and designers deeply understand their customer. They spend tremendous energy developing that intuition. They study and understand many anecdotes rather than only the averages you'll find on surveys. They live with the design.

I'm not against beta testing or surveys. But you, the product or service owner, must understand the customer, have a vision, and love the offering. Then, beta testing and research can help you find your blind spots. A remarkable customer experience starts with heart, intuition, curiosity, play, guts, taste. You won't find any of it in a survey.

Embrace External Trends

Amazon is testing its grocery store powered by Artificial Intelligence in Seattle.

The outside world can push you into Day 2 if you won't or can't embrace powerful trends quickly. If you fight them, you're probably fighting the future. Embrace them and you have a tailwind.

These big trends are not that hard to spot (they get talked and written about a lot), but they can be strangely hard for large organizations to embrace. We're in the middle of an obvious one right now: machine learning and artificial intelligence.

Over the past decades, computers have broadly automated

tasks that programmers could describe with clear rules and algorithms. Modern machine learning techniques now allow us to do the same for tasks where describing the precise rules is much harder.

At Amazon, we've been engaged in the practical application of machine learning for many years now. Some of this work is highly visible: our autonomous Prime Air delivery drones; the Amazon Go convenience store that uses machine vision to eliminate checkout lines; and Alexa, our cloud-based AI assistant. (We still struggle to keep Echo in stock, despite our best efforts. A high-quality problem, but a problem. We're working on it.)

But much of what we do with machine learning happens beneath the surface. Machine learning drives our algorithms for demand forecasting, product search ranking, product and deals recommendations, merchandising placements, fraud detection, translations, and much more. Though less visible, much of the impact of machine learning will be of this type—quietly but meaningfully improving core operations.

Inside Amazon Web Services, we're excited to lower the costs and barriers to machine learning and AI so organizations of all sizes can take advantage of these advanced techniques.

Using our pre-packaged versions of popular deep learning frameworks running on P2 compute instances (optimized for this workload), customers are already developing powerful systems ranging everywhere from early disease detection to increasing crop yields. And we've also made Amazon's higher-level services available in a convenient form. Amazon Lex (what's inside Alexa), Amazon Polly, and Amazon Recognitions remove the heavy lifting from natural language understanding, speech generation, and image analysis. They can be accessed with simple API calls—

no machine learning expertise required. Watch this space. Much more to come.

High-Velocity Decision-Making

Day 2 companies make high-quality decisions, but they make high-quality decisions slowly. To keep the energy and dynamism of Day 1, you have to somehow make high-quality, high-velocity decisions. Easy for startups and very challenging for large organizations. The senior team at Amazon is determined to keep our decision-making velocity high. Speed matters in business—plus a high-velocity decision-making environment is more fun too. We don't know all the answers, but here are some thoughts.

First, never use a one-size-fits-all decision-making process. Many decisions are reversible, two-way doors. Those decisions can use a light-weight process. For those, so what if you're wrong? I wrote about this in more detail in last year's letter.

Second, most decisions should probably be made with somewhere around 70% of the information you wish you had. If you wait for 90%, in most cases, you're probably being slow. Plus, either way, you need to be good at quickly recognizing and correcting bad decisions. If you're good at course correcting, being wrong may be less costly than you think, whereas being slow is going to be expensive for sure.

Third, use the phrase "disagree and commit." This phrase will save a lot of time. If you have conviction on a particular direction even though there's no consensus, it's helpful to say, "Look, I know we disagree on this but will you gamble with me on it? Disagree and commit?" By the time you're at this point, no one can know the answer for sure, and you'll probably get a quick yes.

This isn't one way. If you're the boss, you should do this too. I disagree and commit all the time. We recently greenlit a particular Amazon Studios original. I told the team my view: debatable whether it would be interesting enough, complicated to produce, the business terms aren't that good, and we have lots of other opportunities. They had a completely different opinion and wanted to go ahead. I wrote back right away with "I disagree and commit and hope it becomes the most watched thing we've ever made." Consider how much slower this decision cycle would have been if the team had actually had to convince me rather than simply get my commitment.

Note what this example is not: It's not me thinking to myself "well, these guys are wrong and missing the point, but this isn't worth me chasing." It's a genuine disagreement of opinion, a candid expression of my view, a chance for the team to weigh my view, and a quick, sincere commitment to go their way.

And given that this team has already brought home 11 Emmys, 6 Golden Globes, and 3 Oscars, I'm just glad they let me in the room at all!

Fourth, recognize true misalignment issues early and escalate them immediately.

Sometimes teams have different objectives and fundamentally different views. They are not aligned. No amount of discussion, no number of meetings will resolve that deep misalignment. Without escalation, the default dispute resolution mechanism for this scenario is exhaustion. Whoever has more stamina carries the decision.

I've seen many examples of sincere misalignment at Amazon over the years. When we decided to invite third party sellers to compete directly against us on our own product detail pages—that was a big one. Many smart, well-intentioned Amazonians were simply not at all aligned with the direction. The big decision set up hundreds of smaller decisions, many of which needed to be escalated to the senior team.

"You've worn me down" is an awful decision-making process. It's slow and de-energizing. Go for quick escalation instead—it's better.

So, have you settled only for decision quality, or are you mindful of decision velocity too? Are the world's trends tailwinds for you? Are you falling prey to proxies, or do they serve you? And most important of all, are you delighting customers? We can have the scope and capabilities of a large company and the spirit and heart of a small one. But we should choose it.

A huge thank you to each and every customer for allowing us to serve you, to our shareowners for your support, and to Amazonians everywhere for your hard work, your ingenuity, and your passion.

As always, I attach a copy of our original 1997 letter. It remains Day 1.

Sincerely,

Jeff

Appendix C
The Solution

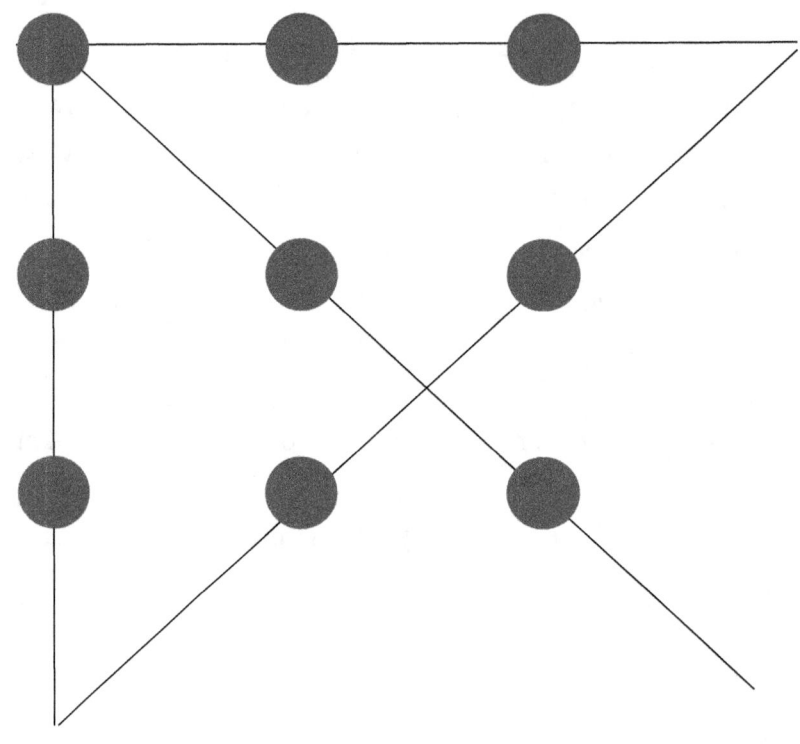

End Notes

[1] Ronald E. Martell, *Showdown in the Pacific War: Nimitz and Yamamoto* (Bloomington, Indiana: Xlibris Press), March 6, 2015.

[2] James F. Dunnigan , and Raymond M. Macedonia, *Getting It Right: American Military Reforms After Vietnam to the Gulf War and Beyond*, (New York City: William Morrow & Co; 1st edition), November 1, 1993.

[3] Blake Ellis, "Bank of America to charge $5 monthly debit card fee," *CNN Money*, September 29, 2011, https://money.cnn.com/2011/09/29/pf/bank_of_america_debit_fee/index.htm.

[4] "Wells Fargo will pay $190 million to settle customer fraud case," *CNBC.com*, September 8, 2016, https://www.cnbc.com/2016/09/08/wells-fargo-reaches-185m-settlement-to-settle-secret-account-fraud-case.html.

[5] Dana Milbank, "Wells Fargo: Too Big to Fail, Too Arrogant to Admit It," *Washington Post,* September 20, 2016, https://www.washingtonpost.com/opinions/wells-fargo-too-big-to-fail-too-arrogant-to-admit-it/2016/09/20/5c7ee1fe-7f6e-11e6-9070-5c4905bf40dc_story.html.

[6] Charles A. O'Reilly III, and Michael L. Tushman, "The Ambidextrous Organization," *Harvard Business Review,* April 2004 issue.

[7] Lizzy Gurdus, "Marc Benioff: We bought Time Magazine because 'business is the greatest platform for change'," *MAD MONEY,* September 25, 2018, https://www.cnbc.com/2018/09/25/benioff-bought-time-because-business-is-greatest-platform-for-change.html.

[8] Olin School of Business at Washington University, "15 years to extinction," *www.cnbc.com*, June 5, 2014.

[9] Lawrence Mishel, and Julia Wolfe *"CEO compensation has grown 940% since 1978," Economic Policy Institute,* August 14, 2019, www.epi.org/publication/ceo-compensation-2018/Report.

[10] "A Decade of Facts and Figures," *Postal Facts*, September 2019, https://facts.usps.com/table-facts/.

[11] George Jensen, "The imminent death of the Postal Service," *The American Interest Online Paper,* https://www.the-american-interest.com/2009/07/01/the-imminent-death-of-the-u-s-postal-service/.

[12] Lisa Rayle, Danielle Dai, Nelson Chan, Robert Cervero, and Susan Shaheen, "Just a better taxi? A survey-based comparison of taxis, transit, and ridesourcing services in San Francisco," *Transport Policy Journal,* Vol. 45, January 2016, pp. 168-178.

[13] "Blockbuster," *Wikipedia,* https://simple.wikipedia.org/wiki/Blockbuster, accessed June 1, 2020.

[14] Chunka Mui, "How Kodak Failed," *Forbes,* January 18, 2012, https://www.forbes.com/sites/chunkamui/2012/01/18/how-kodak-failed/#4e59fd846f27.

[15] "20 STRATEGIC CHANGE RANKINGS FOR 2019," Innosight, *The Transformation 20,* https://www.innosight.com/wp-content/uploads/2019/09/Innosight-Transformation-20-Final.pdf.

[16] Vincent Barabba, *The Decision Loom: A Design for Interactive Decision-Making in Organizations* (Chicago: Triarchy Press Ltd, November 24, 2011).

[17] James M. Burns, *Leadership* (New York: Harper Perennial Political Classics, March 30, 2010).

[18] "Doritos Locos Taco Sales Pass $1 Billion," *Huffington Post,* June 10, 2020, https://www.huffpost.com/entry/doritos-locos-tacos-sales-pass-1-billion_n_5b5716e6e4b01e373aac18d6.

[19] "Ally Financial acquires robo-adviser TradeKing for $275 million," *Investment News,* April 1, 2016, https://www.investmentnews.com/ally-financial-acquires-robo-adviser-tradeking-for-275-million-67025.

[20] "How I Did It: Sammy Hagar," *Inc.,* November 2013, https://www.inc.com/magazine/201311/liz-welch/sammy-hagar.html.

[21] John Haltiwanger, "America's 'war on terror' has cost the US nearly $6 trillion and killed roughly half a million people, and there's no end in sight," *Business Insider*, November 14, 2018, https://www.businessinsider.com/the-war-on-terror-has-cost-the-us-nearly-6-trillion-2018-11.

22
https://en.wikipedia.org/wiki/United_States_military_casualties_in_the _War_in_Afghanistan, Accessed June 8, 2020.

[23] "IMMEDIATE RELEASE: DOD Releases Fiscal Year 2021 Budget Proposal," *U.S. Dept. of Defense*, February 10, 2020, https://www.defense.gov/Newsroom/Releases/Release/Article/20794 89/dod-releases-fiscal-year-2021-budget-proposal/.

[24] Robert Strohmeyer, "The 7 Worst Tech Predictions of All Time," *PC World*, December 31, 2008, https://www.pcworld.com/article/155984/worst_tech_predictions.html.

www.ingramcontent.com/pod-product-compliance
Lightning Source LLC
Chambersburg PA
CBHW070325220526
45467CB00001B/37